The Idle Parent

Why Laid-back Parents Raise

Happier and Healthier Kids

Tom Hodgkinson

JEREMY P. TARCHER/PENGUIN

a member of Penguin Group (USA) Inc.

New York

JEREMY P. TARCHER/PENGUIN
Published by the Penguin Group
Penguin Group (USA) Inc., 375 Hudson Street, New York, New York 10014,
USA • Penguin Group (Canada), 90 Eglinton Avenue East, Suite 700,
Toronto, Ontario M4P 2Y3, Canada (a division of Pearson Penguin
Canada Inc.) • Penguin Books Ltd, 80 Strand, London WC2R 0RL,
England • Penguin Ireland, 25 St Stephen's Green, Dublin 2, Ireland
(a division of Penguin Books Ltd) • Penguin Group (Australia),
250 Camberwell Road, Camberwell, Victoria 3124, Australia (a division
of Pearson Australia Group Pty Ltd) • Penguin Books India Pvt Ltd,
11 Community Centre, Panchsheel Park, New Delhi–110 017, India
• Penguin Group (NZ), 67 Apollo Drive, Rosedale, North Shore 0632,
New Zealand (a division of Pearson New Zealand Ltd)
• Penguin Books (South Africa) (Pty) Ltd,
24 Sturdee Avenue, Rosebank, Johannesburg 2196, South Africa

Penguin Books Ltd, Registered Offices: 80 Strand, London WC2R 0RL, England

Most Tarcher/Penguin books are available at special quantity discounts for bulk purchase
for sales promotions, premiums, fund-raising, and educational needs. Special books or book
excerpts also can be created to fit specific needs. For details, write Penguin Group (USA) Inc.
Special Markets, 375 Hudson Street, New York, NY 10014.

ISBN 978-1-58542-800-7

Printed in the United States of America
1 3 5 7 9 10 8 6 4 2

BOOK DESIGN BY AMANDA DEWEY
INTERIOR ILLUSTRATIONS BY NATHAN BURTON

This publication is designed to provide accurate and authoritative information in regard to the subject
matter covered. It is sold with the understanding that the publisher is not engaged in rendering legal,
accounting, or other professional services. If you require legal advice or other expert assistance, you
should seek the services of a competent professional.

Neither the publisher nor the author is engaged in rendering professional advice or services to the
individual reader. The ideas, procedures, and suggestions contained in this book are not intended as
a substitute for consulting with your physician. All matters regarding your health require medical
supervision. Neither the author nor the publisher shall be liable or responsible for any loss or damage
allegedly arising from any information or suggestion in this book.

For Arthur, Delilah Rose and Henry

Contents

Introduction

How to begin to educate a child. First rule, leave him alone.
Second rule, leave him alone. Third rule, leave him alone.

D. H. LAWRENCE, "Education of the People," 1918

An unhealthy dose of the work ethic is threatening to wreck childhood. Under tyrannical work-obsessed governments, years that should be devoted to play and joyful learning are being stifled by targets and tests and long school hours. Kids' leisure time is invaded by commercial interests in the form of fun sellers and computer games. Pushy parents don't help by making childhood into a stress-filled period of anxious striving and competing. Our kids' days are crammed full with adult-organized activities: ballet, judo, tennis, piano, sports fixtures, art projects. At home kids are entertained by giant screens and computers. In between they are strapped into confining cars and forced to listen to educational tapes. Ambitious mothers force hours of homework on bewildered ten-year-olds, hanging the abstract fear of "future employers" over their heads. Then they buy them a Nintendo Wii, the absurd and costly gadget that is supposed to bring some element of physicality into computer games. It's only a matter of time before kids with busy schedules will have their own BlackBerrys.

What happened to play? I think of the *New Yorker* cartoon that showed two kids in the playground, each staring at his personal organizer. One is saying to the other: "I can fit you in for unscheduled play next Thursday at four."

All these activities impose a huge burden of cost and time on the already harried parent. They leave no time for simply goofing off, for free play. They have the other unwelcome side effect of making children incapable of looking after themselves. When they are stimulated by outside agencies, whether that be a teacher, computer or television, children lose the ability to create their own games. They forget how to play. I remember when our eldest child, a victim of chronic overstimulation by his anxious parents, screamed: "I ... need ... some ... *entertainment!*" in a bored moment. A chilling comment, particularly from a five-year-old. What now? What next? These are the questions our hyper-stimulated kids ask. What has happened to their own imagination, to their own resources?

There is a way out of this overzealous parenting trap. There is a simple solution that will make your life easier and cheaper. It will make your kids' lives more enjoyable and also help to produce happy, self-sufficient children who can create their own lives without depending on a mummy substitute. I call it idle parenting, and our mantra is simply: "Leave them alone." The very welcome discovery that a lazy parent is a good parent was rooted in me by the following passage from a D. H. Lawrence essay, published in 1918, called "Education of the People": "How to begin to educate a child. First rule, leave him alone. Second rule, leave him alone. Third rule, leave him alone. That is the whole beginning."

To the busy modern parent, this idea seems counterintuitive. Aren't we always being told to do more, not less? All parents wander round with a nagging sense that somehow we are doing it all wrong, and that more work needs to be done. Well, no. The problem is that we are putting too much work into parenting, not too little. By overinterfering, we are not allowing the kids to grow up and learn by themselves. The children who have been too much looked after will not know how to look after themselves. We need to retreat. Let them live. Welcome to the school of inactive parenting. It's a win-win situation: less work for you and better for your children, in terms of their enjoying their everyday lives and also for their self-reliance and independence.

Now, I am not, of course, advocating slobbish neglect. Maybe I went too far with my idle parenting when I dozed off on the sofa in front of the wood-burning stove while "doing the child care," as the ugly modern phrase has it, to be woken by the screams of a toddler who had placed his hands squarely on the hot metal and burned his fingertips. Clearly we don't let our children jump out of windows or go about with unchanged diapers. There is carefree and there is careless, and there is a difference.

But to create a household free of care: that would be a wonderful thing. It's been obvious to me watching our three kids grow up that the more they have been ignored, the better. The eldest had a surfeit of anxious parental supervision and is still the trickiest. The second had a little less attention, and she is more self-sufficient. Finally, the third was born on the bathroom floor and has had to get on with his own life.

And he is perhaps the best of all three at playing. Certainly he is the most comical.

The great thing about children is that they like being busy. Since parents like being lazy, it makes sense for the children to do the work. This idea was partly explored in the nineteenth century, when children as young as five were sent into the manufactories. The fact that meddlesome liberals have since introduced child-labor laws need not prevent the idle parent exploiting their own offspring.

I remember my friend John lying in a hammock one sunny afternoon in our garden. He successfully manipulated his four-year-old daughter into bringing him a beer and his cigarettes while he lay there. Yes, it's a little-known fact that much can be achieved by lying down. Simply by doing nothing, you can train children to do useful things. During the most recent school holiday, we found we were lying in bed till ten or eleven. My brother has done even better. One morning he and his wife were lying in bed when their eight-year-old son came in. "Well done," he said. "It's your new record. It's twelve." When kids are abandoned, they teach themselves how to get up, make themselves breakfast and play.

Paradoxically, the idle parent is a responsible parent because at the heart of idle parenting is respect for the child, trust in another human being. It is the irresponsible parent who hands the child over to various authorities for education and care, whether these be child-care providers, schools, after-school clubs, sports teams, the Disney Channel, Nickelodeon or whatever. Or tries to impose their own vision on the children and does not simply let them be.

Now, another great advantage of idle parenting is that it avoids the stimulation of resentment in the parent. There is nothing so corrosive or pestilent as resentment stewing in the breast. Imagine making all those sacrifices, putting yourself out for your children, going without—and then they turn round and go junkie on you in some kind of Amy Winehouse / Pete Doherty nightmare. No, there is no room for martyrs in the world of the idle parent. Our happiness comes first. And that is the right way round; as a cabdriver said to me the other day of his kids: "They're happy because we're happy." Do not suffer. Enjoy your life.

The idle parent is a stay-at-home parent. Not for us a host of costly leisure pursuits at the weekend. We reject the costly thrills of antiseptic plastic fun palaces, zoos, theme parks and family days out in general. We sit on the sofa and let things happen and find fun in our own backyards. We make airplanes out of cereal boxes. It's amazing how many catching and tickling games you can play with your kids while sitting on the sofa. We have one called Tickle or Trap: the child runs toward me, yells "Tickle!" or "Trap!" and I carry out his instruction. Much hilarity.

The idle parent is a thrifty parent. We don't work too hard and therefore we can't expect to be rolling in cash. And with thrift comes creativity. "Thrift is poetic because it is creative," as the great thunderer G. K. Chesterton wrote, "waste is unpoetic because it is waste." When you sit around at home with no money, you start to discover your own inner resources. You make things and draw. Put a pile of paper on the kitchen table, along with a stapler, scissors, crayons and glue, and you'll be amazed at what your children come up with. Forget LeapPads and digital gadgets. Go analogue. It's more fun and it's a lot cheaper. Put a bird feeder outside the kitchen window. Fun does not have to be expensive.

We don't care about status and career advancement and how we are perceived by others. We are free of all of that rubbish. We simply want to enjoy our lives and to give our children a happy childhood. What greater gift could there be from a parent? If our children will say, "I enjoyed my childhood," to their friends, then I would count that as a great achievement. Better to have a happy childhood than a high-achieving one with a huge shrink bill to pay in adult life.

The idle parent is sociable. We recognize the importance of friends. Friends lighten the burden. One of the myths of modern society is the idea that "you're on your own in this world." Instead of talking to friends and neighbors, anxious moderns seek advice in books and websites and Internet forums. We try to do everything ourselves and resist asking for help or admitting weakness to others. No! Be weak! Give up! You can't do everything. Lower your standards. Get friends to come and help you. Organize little get-togethers at your house where parents can chat and kids can play. Ignore the children. I love D. H. Lawrence's idea of child care. He says babies should "be given to stupid fat old women who can't be bothered with them . . . leave the children alone. Pitch them out into the streets or the playgrounds, and take no notice of them." Do not view them as raw material to be molded into obedient slaves for the workplace of the future. Let them play. And yes, get your friends involved. Life is so much easier when the work is shared. Friends bring laughter and joy. No sadder sight than the lone parent, pushing her child around the gloomy municipal park, trying to tell herself that she is having a good time.

My idea of child care is a large field. At one side of the field is a marquee with a bar serving local ales. This is where the parents gather. On the other side of the field, somewhere in the distance, the children play. I don't bother them, and they don't bother me. Give them as much freedom as possible.

But the life of an idle parent is not always easy. Children do not always adapt to the anticonsumerist model that the natural parent promotes. They want stuff. Children get in your face. They make a terrible mess. They scream and whine. And the mother and father seem to disagree on pretty much everything, from paint colors to mealtime manners, as a matter of marital policy. And there are more worries. Is it mean to deny your kids an iPod Nano or Nintendo Wii and give them a ball of string and *The Dangerous Book for Boys* for their birthday instead? Should I really put a broadband connection in the tree house? Should I put more hours in at the office so they can go on skiing holidays and wear expensive sneakers? Would I be less grumpy if I drank less alcohol? Sometimes we doubt our own gospel. So I hope to outline an enjoyable parenting philosophy in these pages, while also acknowledging that it ain't always easy. I will confess my many and various parenting errors. I am a disaster-prone and chaotic layabout, and so should warn you not to listen to my advice. Certainly my friends think that the idea of me advising other parents on child-care issues is absurd.

With that caveat in mind, let us go forth, throw away the rule books, forget what other people think, and enjoy family life and all its joys and woes.

When preparing this book I deliberately avoided reading any of the modern child-care gurus, since it is precisely the modern orthodoxy that I think is causing the problems. Instead, I have gone back to two of our greatest philosophers from more reflective times, John Locke, of the seventeenth century, and Jean-Jacques Rousseau, of the eighteenth century. Both seem to me to provide admirable thoughts and ideas for raising children. Locke published *Some Thoughts Concerning Education* in 1693, and Rousseau published his guide to "natural" education, *Émile*, in 1762. His idea was to "shield [the child] from the crushing force of social conventions" and to produce a sort of nature boy.

As much as anything else, the book is a record of my own failures, disasters and mistakes. My friends all laughed when I told them I was writing a child-care guide. They had all seen me blowing my top with small children. So I do not present the words that follow as a smug guide, more a set of reflections that will open up a dialogue and free parents to invent their own approaches to family life rather than try to follow a set of someone else's rules. There are many paths. In rejecting the narrow, singular and uniform vision of life that has been handed down to us by our Puritan forefathers—which sees life as about hard work and moneymaking—we open up a million new paths, and we run into the fields with a new joy, liberated at last.

Tom Hodgkinson
North Devon, England

THE IDLE PARENT MANIFESTO

We reject the idea that parenting requires hard work.

We pledge to leave our children alone.

We reject the rampant consumerism that invades children's lives
from the moment they are born.

We read them poetry and fantastic stories without morals.

We drink alcohol without guilt.

We reject the inner Puritan.

We don't waste money on family days out and holidays.

An idle parent is a thrifty parent.

An idle parent is a creative parent.

We lie in bed for as long as possible.

We try not to interfere.

We play in the fields and forests.

We push them into the garden and shut the door so we can clean
the house.

We both work as little as possible, particularly when the kids are small.

Time is more important than money.

Happy mess is better than miserable tidiness.

Down with school.

We fill the house with music and merriment.

We reject health and safety guidelines.

We embrace responsibility.

There are many paths.

1.

Bring Back Child Labor

Children are much less apt to be idle than men . . .
JOHN LOCKE, *Some Thoughts Concerning Education*, 1693

Work or play are all one to him, his games are his work;
he knows no difference.
JEAN-JACQUES ROUSSEAU, *Émile*, 1762

How often do we hear that children are an encumbrance, a burden? That child care is a regrettable duty, that children must be entertained, fobbed off, looked after? Such are the delusions that we in the West labor under when it comes to raising kids. We see family life as restrictive, busy, work-filled, exhausting, costly. We become slaves to the tiny tyrants. We sigh and moan and wish we had more money.

Well, there is an easy way both to lighten your own load and to help the child feel that he or she has a practical role in the household and in wider society. The phrase "child labor" has an unpleasant ring to it: chimney sweeps, the Industrial Revolution, sweatshops on the other side of the world, the exploitation of powerless urchins to serve the greed of the big-bellied mill owner. But it's time to drop those connotations and get the kids working for you around the house. They like it!

You can start by doing less yourself. Stop trying to be an efficient, hardworking parent. Lie in bed and see what happens. You will find that doing less for your children will make them self-reliant. And remember that in this book we are doing two complementary things: one, we are making life easier for you; and two, we are creating self-reliant, independent children, children who can look after themselves and will not go begging to an employer or other authority figure to look after them. A recent example of this is our son Arthur and the morning tea. Instead of being well-organized automatons, leaping out of bed at 6:30 a.m. to get the breakfast ready, we decided to slumber, to stay in bed. At about nine o'clock a miracle occurred. The bedroom door opened, and in walked an eight-year-old boy with two cups of tea. Oh joy! The boy was clearly loving the fact that he was making a practical contribution to the running of the household, and we, of course, were delighted. Now, if we had been up early, he would never have carried out this important domestic task. It was precisely through us being useless that he became useful. Being a too-good parent, doing too much for my children, I began to see, might result in a chronic lack of self-sufficiency on their part.

Children who have too much done for them cannot do things for themselves. Have you noticed how they expect their parents to know the precise location of all their belongings at any point? "Where's my Game Boy?" the child tyrant whines. "I can't find my socks." Piano practice is done only if there is a parent guiding the child through every step. He needs his hand held, but we have only ourselves to blame. Listen to D. H. Lawrence:

> From earliest childhood, let us have independence, independence, self-dependence. Every child to do all it can for itself, wash and dress itself, clean its own boots, brush and fold its clothes, fetch and carry for itself, mend its own stockings, boy or girl alike, patch its garments, and as soon as possible make as well as mend for itself. Man and woman are happy when they are busy, and children the same.

And the more folding and mending the child can do for itself, the less the adult will have to do for it. It's actually shocking, by the way, to learn from this passage how useless we adults have become since it was written in 1918. After all, what parents today mend their own clothes? As Lawrence warned, the mollycoddling and overprotection of children has created a nation of "big babies." If *we* are dependent and impractical ourselves, then what hope for our children?

Well, there is hope, because we can learn together. We can recapture the lost arts of domestic living. Simple jobs like making bread, jam and preserves can be done with your kids. Kids love

kneading, stirring and licking the bowl. Learn to look after yourself and you will teach your children to look after themselves, and
before too long they will bake bread for you.

And how do we make children help? Lawrence, like Rousseau, was keen to stress that we should not promote a work ethic—
i.e., the idea of work as a necessary suffering—in kids or try to
make them help out of altruism or pity for parents. The purpose
of work, he wrote, is

> not to "help," nor the ethical religious service of mankind. Nor
> is it the greedy piling up of stupid possessions. An individual
> works for his own pleasure and independence: but chiefly in
> the happy pride of personal independence, personal liberty. . . .
> To be free, one must be self-reliant . . . what we want for every
> child is to be handy, physically adaptable and handy.

Do not become a servant to the whims of your materialistic
brats. Instead of eating sweets and slumping in front of the
telly or staring at the computer screen, they should be working.
My New York friend Heather has two young kids, and here is
her view:

> I personally think there should be much more effort put into
> training children to mix martinis and do the housework. If Sam
> does a lot of dusting for me, he gets twenty-five cents pocket
> money. He is very good at getting into the corners, I find. I am
> also pleased that Clementine's potato-chip-handing-out skills
> are coming along.

So let's bring back child labor. And I really believe we should throw out the dishwasher. Instead of using a dishwasher, the whole family should wash up after each meal. One person does the washing, one does the drying and one does the putting away. It takes a mere fifteen minutes. As Woody Guthrie sang, if we all work together, it won't take very long. Put the Monkees on the CD player and the whole thing can turn into a real pleasure. The dishwasher, however, for all its promises of lightening the load, like machinery in general, in actual fact turns washing-up into drudgery. Without it, the children will learn to help, and what's more, they really will make a genuine contribution. They will be useful. And it may help to prevent whining (a tricky problem, which we will explore in greater depth in the next chapter). This is because whining in children results from their sense that they are seen as encumbrances and have nothing to offer. Only the powerless whine. So make them useful!

It's important to remember that the creation of incapable people is at the heart of the industrial-capitalist plot. Incapable people depend on other people, on professionals, on machines, and on money. If you can't do something for yourself, or for yourselves in the case of a family or community, then you will look to the market economy to satisfy your needs for you. So it is that by doing too much for our kids we make them the commodity-dependent adult brats of the future.

In Ivan Illich's lecture "Taught Mother Tongue," given in India in 1978, the great thinker links uselessness and money: "Today, the individual's feelings about his own needs are first associated with an increasing feeling of impotence: in a commodity-dominated environment, needs can no longer be satisfied without recourse to a store, a market." Therefore it has become practically an instinct to spend money, rather in the same way that when in need today we find ourselves almost instinctively reaching for the mouse. The computer, sold as a tool of emancipation, becomes difficult to live without. There is a power outage at home, the broadband connection is lost and the result is a terrible feeling of helplessness. We come to depend on the thing that was supposed to free us. So with money.

We need to return, says Illich, to "self-reliance and trust in others. . . . In a world where 'enough' can be said only when nature ceases to function as pit or trash can, the human being is oriented not toward satisfaction but toward grudging acquiescence."

"That's life," we lie to ourselves. Actually, the "that" that we say life is, grudgingly acquiescing, is not life. It is a travesty of life, life as mere survival.

Women, take heed! Stop working and start living! Mothers work too hard. They get jobs and they work too hard at home as well. Their hard work is bad for their own health and bad for the health of their children, who will grow up weak and dependent and therefore will become willing slaves in the job marketplace.

Capable, self-sufficient, businesslike: men and women should reject slavery to the corporation and grab back control of their own lives by making stuff at home. In the process, children will become useful little helpers, and they too will learn the arts

of self-sufficiency. By working in this way you will start to enjoy
fatherhood and motherhood, rather than suffering it, rather than
grudgingly acquiescing, in Illich's phrase.

When parents make the simple decision to enjoy their child's
company then what we call "child care" ceases to be a burden.
There is a linguistic problem here. We need to ban the phrase
"child care," with its connotations of toil, outsourced and professionalized, and use the word "playing" instead. "Child care" is the
commodification of play. It turns play into something that has to
be paid for. It's all in the mind. If we can make this mental switch,
says Rousseau, then:

> The noisy play of children, which we thought so trying, be-
> comes a delight; mother and father rely more on each other and
> grow dearer to one another; the marriage tie is strengthened.
> In the cheerful home life the mother finds her sweetest duties
> and the father his pleasantest recreation.

When parents do too much, they tire themselves and weaken
their children. Rousseau again:

> The mother may lavish excessive care on her child instead of
> neglecting him; she may make an idol of him; she may develop
> and increase his weakness to prevent him feeling it; she wards
> off every painful experience in the hope of withdrawing him
> from the power of nature, and fails to realize that for every tri-
> fling ill from which she preserves him the future holds in store

many accidents and dangers, and that it is a cruel kindness to prolong the child's weakness when the grown man must bear fatigue.

We must concentrate not on removing pain but on strengthening our ability to deal with pain. Let them fall over and scrape their knees and get wet and muddy. Let them clamber over rocks. There must be danger in life; there must be pain as well as pleasure. "Dip them in the waters of Styx," urges Rousseau in *Émile*.

The conceit of the book is the raising of a fictional creation, Émile, from birth to teenagerhood. It was intended to encourage well-to-do women of the time to get back in touch with their babies. There had been a trend toward the outsourcing of breastfeeding to wet nurses and for mothers to rush back out to enjoy the pleasures of the town, leaving their children with servants. Rousseau hated this shirking of responsibility, but he also warned against overprotection. He wanted mothers to be "natural," for example, to breastfeed their own babies, and the book led to a major vogue in eighteenth-century French society for parents to bring up their kids *"à la Jean-Jacques."*

It ain't easy, though. This is because we live, more than Rousseau, more than Lawrence, in a dependent, overmothered society. I have just returned from the kitchen, where I was trying to force the children to put cutlery and plates away. Yes, they did eventually manage it, but not without a good deal of theatrical panting, deliberately slow walking, pouting, slouching, tutting, sighing, carrying the cutlery awkwardly in their arms and letting it slide to the floor, and with noisy protestations such as "Owah." How they dawdle! It's a continual struggle. They are spoiled. And I need to learn to manipulate rather than try to use my puny authority to coerce them into helping. To escape from a master/ slave duality is crucial, because kids naturally rebel when compelled to do things by authority. And putting "please" on the end of your order somehow makes it worse: it transforms a request into an order under the pretense of being well-mannered. But find a way of making your children contribute, like children in African villages, gutting fish and whittling at the age of five. In a wage economy, rather than a subsistence one, children are more or less useless until they get a job, and therefore school merely fills in the time and gives them the rudiments of an education in order to fit them for some miserable wage employment.

The idle parent is not preparing his or her offspring for the arid and spiritless desert of the corporate workplace. No: this child will be bold, self-sufficient, fearless. He or she will have the courage to be self-employed. So the child will be constantly encouraged to contribute work to the household. We must see the household as a sort of commune, an association of individuals who have come to live together under one roof.

Though this does not mean that the children have equal say: they need to be taught and you are the teacher, so you must take responsibility.

Don't hover around them and ask what they want all the time. I see mothers hovering over two-year-olds like a sycophantic French waiter, saying, "Well, maybe this flavor of juice would suit sir? Would you like one of these?" while the two-year-old shouts

"No" and throws stuff across the room. You are in charge, but you need to create a hierarchy without recourse to authority. As in the old medieval city, the "common good" of the family is paramount. Much of the strife of the modern household comes because we have a selfish Enlightenment view of individuality and freedom in our heads. We see freedom as a matter of asserting our own selfish desire in competition with the selfish desires of others. Enlightenment philosophy has created a nation of self-indulgent egotists, intent on recklessly pursuing every whim. "I really need some me-time"—oh, too sick-making! "Because you're worth it." "It's really important for me." "I need some space." But we are living together, and pleasures should be shared and bread broken together. This is where I part company with Rousseau, who keeps Émile apart from the world. Émile seems to spend twenty-four hours a day with his tutor. Live together. And we must learn to live in the world—by which I mean the world out there, the consumer society, the world of jobs and money and shopping—while remaining unvictimized by it.

These days we create for ourselves an absurd panoply of "likes and dislikes" and call it freedom. It's a commodification of the notion of free will. Instead of behaving as free people and instead of feeling truly alive, we reduce existence to a list of products: "Likes: Red Bull, VW, *The Simpsons*, Apple Mac, Arcade Fire. Dislikes: Dr Pepper, Toyota, *Ugly Betty*, PCs, Metallica." So what? Children pick up on this. They think that when they shout "I HATE pasta," they are asserting their individuality. Well, we're moving toward a situation where family members will sit at the table with a different meal in front of each of them, all wearing iPods transmitting their favorite music into their brains. No talking. Soon we'll have our own little iTVs. (Consider the genius and the evil of the "i" prefix: entertainment you control! It is the fulfillment of the lonely ideals of Puritanism.) All wrong! So says the Third Patriarch of Zen:

> To set up what you like against what you dislike—this is the disease of the mind.
>
> And all too much work and costing too much money! Pleasures and pains should be shared. Let us listen to the same music.

The key is to make work into something enjoyable. Drudge work is lighter when shared and when there's music playing. And you have a responsibility to enjoy your work as well, or else your kids will grow up with the idea of work as simply a necessary burden. Every moan you make will be listened to by those little ears. "Daddy works in a job he hates in order to buy you rubbish to fill your time until the day comes when *you* will work in a job you hate to pay the bills and pay the mortgage."

Why not sing while you wash up? Before the days of radio, we all sang all day long. The streets of medieval cities were lined with craftspeople and traders, all singing their hearts out. This custom persists in the cries of today's street-market traders.

Yes, sing! You must not give your child the idea that work is suffering. That idea will only make it easier for the capitalists to exploit your offspring later. If children are brought up with the idea that work is suffering, then they won't be surprised when they go to work one day and find the experience painful. And that means that employers need make little or no effort to make work joyful. But encourage the idea that all forms of work can be enjoyable and they will naturally create their own path through life rather than dumbly and meekly accepting a future that's been mapped out for them. . . .

One activity that demonstrates that work can be joyful, creative and self-directed is gardening. Here is a magical, mysterious, satisfying, useful, therapeutic and health-giving form of work. Every family should have some sort of garden, or access to one. If you live in a tenth-floor apartment with no windowsill or balcony, get a garden plot nearby. Rousseau recommends gardening to Émile; that great English agitator and promoter of self-sufficiency William Cobbett, in *Rural Rides*, boasts of his son's hoeing abilities. Make a hole, throw a bean into it, watch the plant grow and let the fruit of it be the property of the children.

Rousseau agrees that collapsing the distinction between work and play is essential:

We must never forget that all this should be play, the easy and voluntary control of the movement which nature demands of them, the art of varying their games to make them pleasanter, without the least bit of constraint to transform them into work. . . . Work or play are all one to him, his games are his work; he knows no difference. He brings to everything the cheerfulness of interest, the charm of freedom. . . . Is there anything better worth seeing, anything more touching or delightful, than a pretty child, with merry, cheerful glance, easy contented manner, open smiling countenance, playing at the

most important things, or working at the lightest amusements?

Furthermore, if you can make, for example, putting away toys
or washing-up into a game, then your life will be made easier.
"Who can put most things into the box?" you can ask. I realize now
that my former techniques—shouting, "How many times have I
told you to CLEAR UP THIS BLOODY MESS!" or threatening to
(and then actually) vacuuming up their horrible little toys—were
wrong. You have to get smart. In this way much can be achieved
with very little effort on your part. For example, I can now make
all my children go up to bed without moving from the sofa. I simply make it into a competition: "Who's going to be the first up-
stairs? One, two, three . . ." and they are off, out of the room and
running up the stairs.

Another manipulative technique is recommended by Rousseau. Instead of ordering them to do something, tell them that
you are going to do it and ask if they'd like to join you. I tried
this out this morning and it worked. "I'm going down for breakfast, Arthur. Would you like to join me?" "Yes!" he said, and took
my hand.

We must replace coercion and authoritarian rule with joint
voluntary action. This is the way to make our children free,
autonomous, self-determined, courageous, able to snap their
fingers at government and big business, neither master nor
slave. And to do this, we must learn a few tricks.

2.

Stop the Whining

What wisdom can you find that is greater than kindness? Love
childhood, indulge its sports, its pleasures, its delightful instincts.

Do you know the surest way to make your child miserable?

Let him have everything he wants.

JEAN-JACQUES ROUSSEAU, *Émile*

The great problem for the idle parent is to achieve the right balance between indulgence and discipline. And although Rousseau has been accused of sentimentalizing childhood, he is actually very firm. He is well aware that there is a difference between "a merry child and a spoiled darling." The mission of the idle parent is to let kids play while avoiding spoiling them. This will stop the whining, perhaps the most painful manifestation of our wrongheaded modern parenting techniques.

Why do children moan and whine? Why do they make those dreadful noises? We could start by asking which animals whine. Not many. Most animals simply accept their fate and get on with it. But this is not the case with the domesticated dog. Because pet dogs are so often pampered and accustomed to getting their own way, they whine when they do not get what they want or when they want something that they cannot get for themselves. This whining is an expression of powerlessness and dependence. When you cannot do anything for yourself, when you have come to rely on others to supply your needs and wants, then whining is the impotent response when things go badly. We know this, too, from our own experience as adults in the workplace. When we don't get what we want, we whine and complain to each other. Sometimes the complaining gets results: a bigger office, a promotion. But we are still completely dependent on our bosses. So it is with children. Because they have no freedom and are accustomed to everything being done for them by their slave-parents, they have to whine and wear us down with those unbearable noises to get what they want. So we need to replace the whining with a calm request for help or, better still, train them to resolve their own problems and satisfy their own needs. I am currently trying this out with my own kids. Formerly my approach to their whining would be a shouted comment along the lines of "I can't stand your whining!" or "STOP WHINING! It's driving me crazy!" Of course, such reactions only tend to increase their feelings of self-pity: "Everything was already going wrong," they will be thinking, "and now, to make things worse, Daddy is shouting at me."

So if shouting and swearing, understandable reactions though they might be, don't work, we need to try another approach, bearing in mind at all times that the more independent and self-sufficient the child, the more idle the parent. Idleness is not synonymous with chaos. In fact, efficiency can lead to more idling time. This morning, for example, we achieved a miracle: three children were dressed and breakfasted by eight o'clock, giving us twenty minutes of playtime before the school bus arrived.

Having recently created for ourselves a stressful and chaotic situation in the mornings, with children refusing to get dressed, then missing the bus, necessitating driving to school, we decided to invent a simple routine for morning and evening. I discussed it with the kids and they seemed to think it was acceptable. It went like this, and I pinned it on the kitchen bulletin board so we would be reminded of it. (Victoria, the mother of my children, accuses me of being a fascist, but I argue that chaos is not the same as idleness, and since an easier life is my aim and since chaos makes life stressful, some kind of routine is helpful. Not that we were going to be overly strict in its enforcement. Every day is different, and who knows when we might decide to walk around under the stars and go to bed late one day? Or throw the homework on the fire and take the car downtown, as David Bowie sang?) Anyway, the routine goes like this:

Morning

7:15—Dress

7:45—Breakfast

8:10—Tidy up

8:20—Leave for bus

Evening

6:00—Dinner followed by play

7:00—Bath

7:30—Stories

8:00—Lights-out

This morning, inspired by Rousseau's love of play, I discussed with Arthur the idea of "evening games." Between dinner and bath we will play. Wrestling Time is something most children enjoy, rolling around on the floor, attacking each other and making theatrical grunting noises. Running races around the house are easy for parents, as you simply have to stand or even sit in one place and say, "On your marks, get set, go!" We also enjoy Stair Ball, where the kids stand at the top of the stairs, I stand at the bottom, and each of us has to try to throw the ball past the other and hit a target. Such games are far preferable to the commodities pushed at us by the toy industry. You can take your Pop-Up Pirates and your Hungry Hungry Hippos, with their huge cleaning-up time and mess-making potential, and their unbiodegradable oil-based ugliness, and consign them to the toy chest, or better still, don't buy such vanities in the first place. (We'll return to the problem of toys in a later chapter.) Physical games, though, will tire them out and should help prevent the whining, giving as they do an outlet for the aggressive side of their natures.

We need to impose our routines with a light touch. Otherwise we are in danger of creating factory-ready robots. Rousseau's Émile is a creature of nature and is shielded from industrial work rhythms: "He does not know the meaning of habit, routine and custom; what he did yesterday has no control over what he is doing today; he follows no rule, submits to no authority, copies no pattern, and only acts or speaks as he pleases."

But in order to avoid being a slave to the caprices of the child, we need to be able to look forward to a peaceful evening without the kids, or a chance to go to the pub or see friends. There is nothing worse than collapsing exhausted into bed at 9:30 after spending two hours getting the fiends to bed, and then being woken again at 6:00 a.m. by a toddler jumping on your face.

So a routine, applied with a light touch and flexibility, can be a friend to the Idler. I'm not recommending a von Trapp–style military regime. In any case, this would seem to cause more trouble and woe than it solves, because when oppressed we naturally rebel, and this is what naughtiness is all about, the child making an attempt to bring some autonomy—or even dignity—into its life. Just as skipping work for adults is a way of clawing back some of the dignity we have lost through enslaving ourselves to the corporation, so naughtiness is the child's attempt to resist tyranny. The more tyranny, the more naughtiness. The more rules, the more rules there are to be broken. Naughtiness is an expression of the will to freedom: "I love the imperious nature of children," says my friend Mark Manning (also known as the heavy-metal singer Zodiac Mindwarp). Children resist tyranny at every turn. Do not become a Captain Bligh, ruling through fear, hunger and the lash until the men can see no other option but mutiny.

The other way to cut down the whining is to stop your own. This means getting enough sleep and avoiding stress. In my experience, full-time jobs interrupt sleep to an insupportable degree: there is no siesta time. You have to arrive early at work. The modern workplace also creates stress: most are hellishly pressured places. It's no wonder that the occasional American worker flips and goes into the office or factory with a gun and shoots his co-workers before turning the gun on himself. It's only a matter of time before we get a workplace massacre in Europe. Therefore, the idle parent who wants to stop the whining needs to stop whining himself, and one way is to resist the call to work ever harder and longer hours. Throw your BlackBerry into the river. Unslave yourself. Hard work will not lead to health and happiness. Just ask yourself: would you rather spend your child's first few years playing with them or working for the mega-corp in order to make them profits and you money to buy rubbish you don't need in order to dull the pain of overwork? The mega-corp doesn't need you; the kids do.

Better to be penniless and at home than rich and absent, certainly during the first three or four years of each child's life. There will be plenty of time for hard work for you when they grow up. Your work, I'm afraid, is not particularly important and certainly not as important or as pleasurable as ensuring that your kids enjoy their first years.

This is not to say that between them parents do not need to work and earn some sort of income. They surely do. And the idle parent aims to make the money-earning something enjoyable and creative. So be clever about it. Overwork will kill you. It will wreck your life and your kids' lives. And it will lead to whining— and as we have agreed, the whining must stop.

In order to prevent whining, do not give them everything they ask for. Says Rousseau:

> I have known children brought up like this who expected you to knock the house down, to give them the weather-cock on the steeple, to stop a regiment on the march so that they might listen to the band; when they could not get their way they screamed and cried and would pay no attention to anyone. In vain everybody strove to please them; as their desires were stimulated by the ease with which they got their own way, they set their hearts on impossibilities, and found themselves face to face with opposition and difficulty, pain and grief. Scolding, sulking, or in a rage, they wept and cried all day.

We need to get out of our heads the idea that saying "no" is an act of unkindness. We need to accustom our children to what is and isn't possible from an early age. Perhaps as a result of guilt for overworking, we indulge and spoil our kids, thus creating a whole lot of unnecessary work. The idle parent is motivated by the goals of pleasure and lazing about, and "no" can be an effective tool to serve these ends. Remember that the more idle the parent, the happier the child, because the idle parent is spontaneous: joyful, free of resentment and therefore better company.

Just saying "no," firmly and quietly, and being backed up by the other parent (if there is one) should be a trick that every idle parent masters. It is not the same as cruelty; in fact, it is the very opposite. Saying "no" to the child can also be seen as saying "no" to the forces of branding, toys, money and the whole commodity culture. Rousseau: "Let your 'No,' once uttered, be a wall of brass, against which the child may exhaust his strength some five or six times, but in the end he will try no more to overthrow it."

When you say "no" to *things*, you help your child to become useful and self-sufficient, because saying "no" to *things* is saying "yes" to humanity and "yes" to life. Your child must not grow used to the idea that his or her needs can be met simply by an injection of cash. Then the child will come to want more and more cash, become dependent on money, and have to do all sorts of unpleasant things as an adult in order to get it. Toys break, fade and die, but love lives on. Be strict. We can see the results of the surfeit of consumer products all around us: adults have become spoiled children. We believe we can have whatever we want and, thanks to credit cards, we can have it now. I want, I want, I want. Postpone the pain till later. But this satisfaction of wants leads only to more wants and therefore we remain perpetually unsatisfied. Children teach us the joys of a cardboard box or a pebble or a twig. The other day we took Delilah and a friend to a pebbly beach, and they played for hours harmoniously, making stone circles. Then we went to the shop, outside of which was one of those mechanical rides designed to steal pound coins from our pockets. Cue whining and shouting and arguing over who was to sit in the driver's seat. Commerce leads to inequality and whining. And we must resist the temptation to teach them that a remote-controlled robot is better than a twig. African children rarely cry. I guess that this is for two reasons: one, because they have more control over their lives, and two, because there is less stuff to argue about.

The fact is that you can treat life as a game and be strict as well. It is perfectly possible to be strict with humor. Don't worry, we are not going down the Puritan road. Susanna Wesley, mother of Methodist John, famously wrote to her son in 1732 advising him that children should "fear the rod and cry softly." The Puritan conception of childhood was that children were sinful, lazy and mischievous, that they were vipers, and that therefore a lot of interfering was required from parents and teachers to correct their evil tendencies. *The Office of Christian Parents*, a parenting guide for the pious, published in 1616, called children "idle . . . vile and abject persons, liars, thieves, evil beasts, slow bellies and good for nothing." Putting aside the harried parent's reaction that they may have had a point, we utterly reject the "sinful" model of childhood, as we utterly reject the "sinful" model of adulthood. Indeed, we need to go beyond good and evil. Rousseau attempts to avoid teaching Émile about such dualities, arguing, for example, that so-called moral fables in fact introduce the child to evil (and in the process tend to make the evildoers the more attractive characters. Who wants to be Miss Goody Two-shoes?). "What's guilt?" Arthur asked me the other day. Well, to explain guilt you would have to introduce the idea of doing bad things and then feeling bad about them later. Since I don't believe in guilt anyway, I thought it better to avoid the whole issue and I replied: "Oh, nothing. Just a silly adult thing."

Rousseau analyzes a fable about a fox, which aims to prove that lying gets you into trouble. Surely, he seems to be saying, it would be better not to read the child the fable and thus avoid the whole true-false duality in the first place, and even to pretend that there is no such thing as lying. To know good, you need to know bad. To the small child, all is the same. It is we adults who introduce notions of morality at too early an age. The natural child does not know the difference between good and bad and cavorts and frolics and cries in happy innocence of these man-made concepts. If I am not bad, how could I be made better? It was the dastardly Elizabethans who introduced the idea of "Houses of Correction." Before that children were not in need of being corrected, and indeed medieval child-care guides concentrate on the practical aspects of the job. They are medical guides rather than philosophical ones, recommending, for example, that the small child wears a sort of leather helmet to protect it from bumps and falls. It seems that it hadn't occurred to the medieval mind that children can be molded like putty by their elders and betters. They simply left children alone.

Whining and complaining arise from powerlessness. Therefore to stop the whining, we must create powerful children. And this means less interference. I am not interested in creating a certain sort of child for a certain sort of role in society. I am interested in making everyday life enjoyable for both parent and child. We should give up the idea of an ideal or perfect education. Everything else will follow from the simple principle of fun, now. Indeed, attempting to look into the future is one of the most dangerous habits when it comes to kids, whose every instinct is to remain gloriously in the present.

So, learn to say "no." Avoid situations that are likely to lead to whining, especially any place where money will change hands, whether the shops, the fair or the ice cream stand. Stay away from

McDonald's, Walmart, Toys "Я" Us. Keep out of the car. Do not confine your children. Leave them alone!

And always remember that the more powerful of spirit your children are, the less likely they are to whine. So set a good example and do not whine and moan yourself. The method is simple; again we say: Leave them alone.

3.

Seek Not Perfection, or Why Bad Parents Are Good Parents

One in All, All in One—if only this is realized.
No more worry about your not being perfect.

THIRD PATRIARCH OF ZEN, d. 606

There are many different styles of parenting. In Papua New Guinea, kids have many mothers. People look after one another's children. Seven-year-olds move hut and go to live with another family. In Sparta, weak babies were left to die on the hillsides. In Plato's *Republic*, where women and men are equal, women are not required to raise their own children, who are instead sent to state nurseries. In the old Norse world, well-off widows often had their children fostered. The practice of wet-nursing was common in Europe until modern times. Today in India or Mexico or rural Africa, families are extended and everyone helps with the child care. The sculptor Barbara Hepworth sent her triplets to a nursery training college in Hampstead because she wanted to make art undisturbed. After the Second World War, two million mothers brought up their kids without a dad. Today, fathers are taking a more active role in helping with the domestic tasks.

I offer these reflections in order to prove the point that historically, philosophically and socially there are many different conceptions of what being a parent is all about, and probably one of the least common is the lonely, stay-at-home mother of the Western imagination. Things do not have to be like this. You can choose your own way.

Motherhood is not a role. It should not actually be a full-time job. The children don't need so much mothering. It has become a full-time job in the West—more than full-time—since we have become so very isolated. Today, we commonly see family life where the husband leaves at 8:00 a.m. and returns at 7:00 p.m. and all the company the mother has during the day is a washing machine and daytime television. The boredom of the young mother is life-wrecking, mad-making. I remember Victoria calling me at my office in tears of desperation when our eldest child was small. I now wish I had spent a lot more time at home during those first two years.

The boredom of the full-time mother is compounded by her guilt: she feels guilty because she is not enjoying the company of her own baby, her own children. She feels a failure for not enjoying motherhood. How far short she falls of the ideal of motherhood presented in magazines and television ads. Why can she not

enjoy herself, like the celebrities who constantly crow on magazine covers about the joys of parenting? Because—I say again—
motherhood is a myth and woman was not made to shop, clean
and burble at baby all day on her own. She needs to combine
motherhood with other creative activities and sociability. The
non-working mother is another myth, or at least the invention of
the Victorian imagination: it was then a sort of status symbol to
have a swooning, trussed-up, inactive wife. But this is an anom-
aly. Everywhere else in the world, and in history, women have
worked. They have worked alongside their husbands in the fields;
medieval woman was equal to man in this respect. Women were
beer brewers, bread bakers, gardeners, businesswomen:

> She sets her mind on a field, then she buys it; with what her
> hands have earned she plants a vineyard.
>
> She puts her back into her work and shows how strong her
> arms can be. . . .
>
> She makes her own quilts, she is dressed in fine linen and
> purple. . . .
>
> She weaves materials and sells them, she supplies the
> merchant with sashes.

So says "The Perfect Housewife," the charming poem that
concludes the Proverbs in the Old Testament (New Jerusalem
edition).

So the idle mother does not actually avoid work. On the
contrary, like the idle father, she embraces it. Work of her own
choosing, that is, independent work, autonomous work, creative

work. What she avoids is that terrible, fearful, spirit-sapping invention of the industrial age: the full-time job. What she avoids is the terrible slavery of the corporation. For the idle mother, it is not a choice between "going back to work" or "staying at home." She explores that vast and rich territory between those two barren poles. She creates her own job, one that she can fit around her children or even stop doing for a few years. And having made the conscious decision to both work and look after the children, she enjoys both. It is our habit of seeing life as a series of burdens imposed on us by outside forces that creates misery. Once we recognize that we are free and responsible creatures, the burden is lifted. We must smash artificial dualisms.

My wife, Victoria, or V as I call her, for example, has made the existential decision to enjoy playing with her children. She doesn't play with them in those life-draining, spirit-sapping hellholes called playgrounds; she plays with them on the floor at home. When we employ others to look after our kids, we tend to make "child care" into a burden. I know this from experience. For three years we employed a full-time nanny. (How did we afford it? Remortgaging. We went into debt, and that gives you an idea of how desperate for help we had become.) And in a sense, it did work: because, isolated as we were, having a nanny was a way of creating an extended family. (By the way, have you noticed how today's globe-trotting grandparents are too busy to babysit? I have been sorely disappointed by my own parents' reluctance to help out in our household.) V did a little paid work, but mostly she was at home with kids and nanny. But after three years we realized that we had started to depend on Claire. She was wonderful, very special, a fantastic person. And she seemed to be so much better with the children than we were. That could make us feel inadequate by comparison. "Your kids are naughty with you and good with her," a friend pointed out. "That's not good for you as a family." We realized that he was right: we had come to dread weekends when Claire was not working and to long for Monday mornings when she would return. So that arrangement came to an end and we did everything on our own for a year. The house was less tidy, but the year on our own was effective in creating a sense of responsibility, confidence and indeed pleasure in ourselves as parents.

Many mothers in the West behave oddly. They talk about their disapproval of women who "go back to work" while complaining about "having to" look after children and constantly shuffling them off to nurseries or child-care centers or nannies. I'm not so worried about the effect of this on the children, who are after all extremely adaptable and resourceful until we train them in the dark arts of dependence, but on the mothers who have this attitude. For this version of motherhood is a socially constructed concept, a myth. And acknowledging the fact that motherhood is a myth is a liberating realization, since it means that we are all free to do it how we like. All paths are valid. Therefore it is every mother's responsibility to create her own unique version of motherhood. And if that means she works hard, fine. If that means that she lies in bed all day eating chocolate, then also fine. Nancy Mitford may not have been the ideal nurturing mother, but I'd rather have her as a mother than Tabitha Twitchit any day (although I do support the way Tabitha Twitchit turns the kittens out into the garden while she prepares for her tea party). Make your own myth and be confident about it. Find right-mindfulness. The babies will be fine.

The same, of course, is true for fatherhood. Some dads like playing, some do not. There are no rules. The quest for perfection must be abandoned. You have to make your own decisions and be a dad without resentment.

In *Émile*, Rousseau attacks those well-to-do eighteenth-century mothers who sent their babies out to wet nurses. But in some cases, they may not have had the choice; for example, perhaps the mother could not produce milk or the mother died in labor. Or perhaps the mother just wanted to continue some sort of social life. So what? Overmothering is too much work, and in any case can lead to a simpering dependence on the part of the child. The best quality a mother can offer her own children is her own happiness, contentment, felicity, independence. That comes first; that is the priority. I don't mean that she should be a vain and selfish pleasure seeker. I am talking about the importance of what Rousseau calls *amour propre*, self-love of a dignified nature, not *amour de soi-même*, which is selfishness.

Invent your own versions of motherhood and fatherhood. There are no rights or wrongs. It's up to you. But I would certainly advise against that cloying, sickly, sentimental, self-conscious mothering that so often in the West is combined with neglect. Children can get on with it on their own. D. H. Lawrence has some stern words to say on the creed of sentimental mothering:

> Take all due care of him, materially; give him all the care and
> tenderness and wrath; which the spontaneous soul emits; but

always, always, at the very quick, leave him alone. Leave him alone. He is not you and you are not he. He is never to be merged into you nor you into him . . . down with exalted mothers, and down with the exaltation of motherhood, for it threatens the sanity of our race. The relation of mother and child, while it remains natural, is non-personal, non-ideal and non-spiritual . . . babies should invariably be taken away from their modern mothers and given, not to yearning and maternal old maids, but rather to stupid fat women who can't be bothered with them. There should be a league for the prevention of maternal love, as there is a society for the prevention of cruelty to animals . . . leave the children alone. Pitch them into the street or the playgrounds, and take no notice of them.

Let them play. Let them run in gangs. Plant the seedlings in good compost and let nature do the rest!

And mothers and fathers need to invent ways to avoid loneliness. Open your house to others. Put the kids in the front room and leave them alone to play together, while the adults chat and drink wine in the kitchen. A sort of vague idealism has invaded our idea of childhood. We have in our minds the idea of the perfect parent, but perfection can never be attained, partly because we don't know what perfection is. Do not be told what to do. Be responsible. And it's your own mental attitude that must come first. Says Rousseau:

I cannot repeat too often that to control the child one must often control oneself. . . . If only you could let well alone, and get others to follow your example. . . . By doing nothing to begin with, you would end with a prodigy of education.

Keep a light touch on the tiller. Stay in the background, like the ideal ruler in the *Tao Te Ching*, whose people barely realize that they are being governed. Once the children are past the age of one, dads are just as capable of looking after them as mums. And because they seem to be more naturally idle than women, according to our philosophy, men will make good mothers. Men tend to leave the kids alone more readily than the anxious mother, burdened as she is by the commercially produced ideal images of magazines and advertisements.

The cause of the idle mother is not helped either by those complaining female newspaper columnists. They are simply careerist self-promoters who have discovered that complaining pays. So they complain and create complaining in others who follow their example. But the others who follow their example do not get paid for their complaining. They do it for free. So we need columnists who write about how much they enjoy their lives, family and all: not in a saintly, self-sacrificing, affected fashion but in a lazy-and-loving-it style. Ban newspapers and magazines from the house: they are enemies of the idle mother with their overpriced and deceitful fantasies.

Bad parents make good parents. The worse the better. Drink more alcohol. Work less. Do less. Give up. I was once interviewed by people from an American women's magazine, and they were particularly tickled by my line "Kids love a tipsy mom." Drink a glass of wine at bath time.

I'm not saying for a moment that you stop loving, hugging, kissing and praising your children and calling them beautiful and wonderful. But all this will come naturally if you enjoy your life and stop resenting their intrusion. Put the baby in a papoose and go to the garden. Hold on to your pleasures.

Similarly, do not cosset the baby. Both Locke and Rousseau recommend cold baths. And yes, Locke provides further inspiration for idle parents. He came from a thrusting Puritan family and was educated at Westminster School, where he was a friend of Dryden. Despite his occasional attacks on idleness, Locke is a good read: comforting and inspiring. It seems that we had the same problems back in 1693 as we do now: Locke, for example, remarks on "the great dissoluteness of manners [among children], which the world complains of." *Some Thoughts* was one of the inspirations for Rousseau's *Émile* (though Rousseau attacks Locke in various particulars), and like *Émile* it is the source of much good food for thought as we search for a definition of the idle—or fully responsible—parent.

While the medieval age produced many manuals containing advice on the care of babies and small children, I'm not sure whether anyone bothered, like Locke and Rousseau, to set down the principles of an ideal education. Indeed, idealism itself was a sort of by-product of the Protestant revolution, because innate in Protestantism is the idea that you can mold your own destiny and particularly the destiny of your children. With this new idea of man's power to self-define comes the idea that children themselves can be molded like pieces of clay. Nurture, in other words, becomes more important than nature. Locke writes:

"The difference to be found in the manners and abilities of men is owing more to their education than to anything else." Certainly the Puritans took a close interest in bending children to their will.

Locke appears to agree with Rousseau on many practical matters. Both recommend a good helping of liberty. Both oppose excessive civilizing. Clothing should be loose, Locke says. We must avoid "straitjacketing." Similarly, Rousseau can't stand the custom of swaddling. Food should be simple: Locke is in favor of a vegetarian diet for the first three or four years of a child's life. "Abstain from flesh" was the phrase he used. Like Rousseau also, he recommends that children from a young age should grow accustomed to extremes of temperature. Yes, the idle parent is not indulgent. Locke even suggests that parents give their children special leaky shoes:

> Have his shoes so thin that they might leak and let in water whenever he comes near it. . . . And he that considers how mischievous and mortal a thing taking wet in the feet is to those who have been bred nicely, will wish he had, with the poor people's children, gone barefoot; who, by that means, come to be so reconciled by custom to wet their feet that they take no more cold or harm by it than if they were wet in their hands.

Sensible stuff: just think how much whining time, cleaning-boot time and general fuss over wet feet that could be saved with Locke's simple precaution. This apparent harshness concerning wet feet expresses another splendid philosophy. The idle parent is not in the business of making a dandified, civilized, pampered, whining little encumbrance. We are interested in the fleet of foot, the burning flame in the eye, the natural child, the tough, self-sufficient boy and girl. Firstly, because a stray child leads to less work for the parent, but also because children ought to be free. The sole of the shoe actually separates us from nature and from the earth. Wearing shoes is a step toward loneliness and isolation. So let the shoes come off wherever possible, and let the boots leak.

Locke likewise would have the children running about outside: "Another thing that is of great advantage to everyone's health, but especially children's, is to be much in the open air and very little as may be by the fire, even in winter. . . . Thus the body may be brought to bear almost anything."

Other pieces of wisdom from Locke include the need for much sleep and the importance of restricting children's intake of alcohol, which suggests that there were a lot of tipsy kids wandering around seventeenth-century England: "They ought never to drink any strong liquor but when they need it as a cordial and the doctor prescribes it." Drugs for the adults, drugs for the kids. I must say that I think it was a cruel blow to parents when the manufacturers of Calpol removed its drowsy-making ingredient. If there's one thing that modern medicine could do for us, it would be to give us a mild sleeping draft for babies. Maybe I will try beer.

Locke is wary of coddling: "[Parents] love their little ones, and 'tis their duty; but they often, with them, cherish their faults too. They must not be crossed, forsooth; they must be permitted

to have their wills in all things." Like Rousseau, he warns that
such spoiling is bad for the child. It is bad for the parent too: it
is expensive and time-consuming to minister to their every
whim. Locke argues that we are in danger of creating vain little
tyrants: "when the little girl is tricked up in her new gown and
commode, how can her mother do less than teach her to admire
herself, by calling her *her little queen* and *her princess*?" So it is, he
argues, that we ourselves teach the vices, and we live to regret it.
Certainly my six-year-old daughter often looks at me with a little
simpering smile and says in a self-consciously girly voice: "Do I
look pretty?" But how can I complain, when it is we parents ourselves who have taught her these attitudes?

Locke is quick to point out, however, that he does not advocate
severity. "I consider them as children, who must be tenderly used,
who must play, and have playthings." Be strict when the children
are small, he says, and give them more indulgence and liberty as
they grow older. Too often, he says, people do it the other way
round, but: "Imperiousness and severity is but an ill way of treat-
ing men, who have reason of their own to guide them, unless you
have a mind to make your children, when grown up, weary of you,
and secretly to say within themselves, *When will you die, Father?*"

Spoiled children and restrained adolescents: it's a problem
we see everywhere. And being restrained, the adolescents pull yet
more tightly on their leashes and build up a huge head of steam,
which will find an outlet somewhere, sooner or later, often in antisocial forms like vandalism and truancy. But be strict with your
children when they are small and gradually freer as they grow up,
and you will end up with children who are your friends.

In my own case, my mother was strict about bedtimes and the like because she was more interested in her career than in my brother and me. In fact, round our way in 1972, she was known as "the woman who hates babies." As we grew up, we were more or less left alone. But this gave us space to play and to look after ourselves. So my memories of childhood are mostly happy and I never resented my mother for being a career woman. Although I did crumble with embarrassment when she shrieked "Darling!" at me from the other side of the playground, in her Biba skirt and outsize earrings.

Locke is of the view that *"slavish discipline makes a slavish temper."* He also warns against bribing children with "apples or sugar-plums," as that will begin to train them in the values of the consumer society and make little materialists of them:

> When you draw him to do anything that is fit by the offer of money, or reward the pains of learning his book by the pleasure of a luscious morsel; when you promise him a lace cravat or a fine new suit upon the performance of some little tasks; what do you do by proposing these as rewards but allow them to be the good things he should aim at, and accustom him to place his happiness in them?

As idle parents, we want unmaterialistic children, not least because all this stuff that they want demands a considerable amount of work. I keep hearing about mothers who take unpleasant work in factories so that they can buy their sons the expensive sneakers that they have been sold by the ad men.

Start early: do not value money. The less they want, the less you will have to work.

Another nice bit of mothering advice in Locke is to tell the kids off in private and praise them in public. He notices that parents tell their kids off in public in order that they are seen by others to be firm and strict. I do this myself: I tell them off in front of others so I can be seen as a "good" parent. But this humiliates the child. Better to praise them in front of others.

Locke also wants to let them play:

> For all their innocent folly, playing, and childish actions are to be left perfectly free and unrestrained, as far as they can consist with the respect due to those that are present. . . . This gamesome humor, which is wisely adapted to their age and temper, should rather be encouraged, to keep up their spirits and improve their strength and health, than curbed or restrained: and the chief art is to make all that they do sport and play too.

Like the Taoists, Locke recommends keeping your rules to an absolute minimum: "Let your rules to your son be as few as is possible."

Recently V left our youngest two children with me and the au pair while she took the eldest on a ten-day holiday. Her traveling companion had left her own one-year-old twins at home with a nanny, her mother and her husband. Far from being traumatized, those children, while their mother was away, stopped waking at night and became less prone to tantrums and grumbling. "I don't know what I was doing, but I know it was my fault," said their mother. It was a similar story with my kids: it's true that the smallest cried out, "Come back, Mummy! Come back, Mummy!" when I put him to bed on the first night, but after that he adjusted and both children were less whiny than usual.

So if you have problems, mothers, with your child's sleeping, then fight against our sentimental conditioning and take a break. Go away for a week. See friends. Drink. Get some sleep. The babies will be fine. In fact, they will benefit from the break. It will help them to break the apron strings. You are not as important as you think: the mothering role can be taken up by people who are not the real mother. Think of adoption and fostering. And all those babies whose mothers died in childbirth. My own mother was really brought up by her grandmother, as her own mother was busy running a flower shop. Ukrainian women today leave their two-year-olds with their mothers while they seek their fortunes in Western Europe. Chinese children are often brought up by their grandmothers. Are we to restrain these mothers' freedom by forcing them to stay at home, imposing our own sickly senti-mental morality on other people?

Give your kids a break. Give yourself a break. Do not suffocate them and do not allow yourself to be suffocated. In any case, you may well not feel endless undying devotion and maternal gooey-ness for your baby. Many women, conditioned by the lies of mag-azines in which highly paid actresses gush about the wonders of motherhood, expect that they are going to fall in love with their babies, and then become clinically depressed if they don't.

Children can adapt to all sorts of mothering styles: there is no best way, and the idea of a "best way" is generally promoted by the representatives of the oligarchy. For example, in Britain and the United States today, women are encouraged to take full-time jobs while they put their babies in nurseries. Not so long ago, they were encouraged to stay at home while men went out to earn the wages. In both cases there is no absolute morality involved, merely a piece of economic expediency dressed up as an ethical code. These decisions are up to the parents, and as long as children have plenty of love around, then they can adapt to virtually anything. We should all stop beating ourselves up: there is no ideal mother and the very idea of a perfect mother is a tyrannical concept used as a method of control by the people in power. I'm an anti-idealist: the very notion of an ideal immediately invites failure because by definition we can never live up to it.

You don't even need to go to the effort of telling them off about minor issues such as table manners. Says Locke: "Never trouble yourself about those faults in them which you know age will cure.... Manners ... are rather to be learned by example than rules; and then children, if kept out of ill company, will take a pride to behave themselves prettily." So let the children make up their own minds to behave well, rather than behaving well under fear of authority. "Fear not, the ornaments of conversation and the outside of fashionable manners will come in their due time." Locke warns against that habitual nagging that parents tend to oppress their children with. He says that to "rate them thus at every turn is not to teach them, but to vex and torment them to no purpose." I think about my own mistakes with my eldest son. I feel that I have vexed and tormented the poor boy to no purpose many times, shouting at him to use the knife and fork properly or stop wriggling in his seat or slumping at mealtimes. Maybe I should ignore these minor misdemeanors. What am I doing by nagging him so? Locke is right. We waste an inordinate amount of time and energy in attempting to correct faults that, given time, will correct themselves. And the idle parent is above all a conserver of energy. We do not exert ourselves when it is pointless or harmful to do so.

4.

The Importance of Nature

Let Nature be your first teacher.

SAINT BERNARD OF CLAIRVAUX (1090–1153)

We hear that in Norway children do not start school until they are seven. Before that, they are simply taken by teachers into the woods, where they play. In the UK and in the United States, small children waste a lot of time learning about rain forests while sitting inside a classroom, not seeing the natural world that is on their own doorstep. By delegating "nature" to something far away, we forget the wilderness outside our own front doors.

Nature is free, fun and a wonderful teacher. Indeed, one of the intentions of Rousseau in *Émile* was to create the "natural child," uncivilized, free of urban prejudice, bright of eye and bold of countenance. Children bred *"à la Jean-Jacques"* would run free in the woods. Rousseau's Émile is brought up in the countryside, away from the degraded values of the town. Children should be running around outdoors, playing freely, not tied to Gradgrindian desks. These days we not only confine our kids all day in schools, but also confine them in cars on the way home from school, and then confine them to the computer and television when they get home. Manacles and fetters everywhere. We turn child care into a problem of containment. In the olden days, children complained of being stuck in school when the sun was shining, and when the bell rang they ran out into the fields. At the age of eight, I walked a mile to school and back every day without parental supervision. Now when the bell rings an anxious, fearful parent is waiting at the gate, to take the cosseted kid either to some over-organized "activity" or straight home, where he will plug himself into the digital straitjacket of the Internet. He might even "talk to his friends" online. Wow. Now you have to buy a computer and pay for a broadband connection in order to talk to a friend. In the olden days, talking to a friend was free.

Where the man-made world is very expensive, nature is free, physically, mentally, spiritually and financially. Where the man-made world is endlessly frustrating, nature is deeply satisfying. Nature is the great generous opposite of mean and greedy commercial culture. It costs nothing. It looks after itself, or at least needs little tending. And the relationship between nature and man can be a beautiful thing indeed, if we think in terms of working with it rather than conquering it and taming its wild ways. That is the Puritan idea: Pull out the weeds, plant things in straight lines, wipe out pests with chemicals, plough, work, toil and isolate each plant. Conquer nature, subdue it, following what

Aldous Huxley called an "unfortunate remark in Genesis." But the child of idle parents is a wild child.

The convenience of nature as a resource for the idle parent cannot be overstated. This became clear to me as I sat on a rocky beach in North Devon with my friend Ged, while our children played together on the rocks. We noticed that they hadn't hassled us for hours. They were playing without whining or complaining, and without any toys. "Nature doesn't disappoint," said Ged. It provides plenty of pebbles to go round. There will be no fighting over pebbles. This is in direct contrast to the commercial world, which disappoints at every turn. Indeed, disappointment is woven into its very fabric. You drop the ice cream; someone else gets a bigger one; you wanted the pink fishing net; parents are forced to say "no" all the time. The last time I went shopping in town with the kids, I thought I could have saved myself some bother by fixing up a loudspeaker on my head that was programmed to repeat the word "no" every five seconds. Recently on Worthing Beach on the south coast of England, my mother and I noticed that all was harmony when the children played on the beach itself: they played with the stones and shells and the sea. But on reaching the pier, with its shops and rides and temptations, there the whining and pleading started. Disappointments, tears, fighting.

So the idle parent should make a point of taking children to the wildest and most shop-free places they can find. This is a cheap option: no money needs to be shelled out, and the idle parent is a frugal parent, because the less money is needed, the less work is needed. So avoid the shops. They also produce waste, which requires extra work, and the idle parent not only avoids work for himself but avoids creating unnecessary extra work for others. Not long after you have bought the plastic crap, it will be thrown away. Someone has to put your trash bag in a truck, drive it to a dump, and throw it into some toxic hold somewhere. You'll also be following the precepts of Locke and Rousseau, who recommend healthy doses of nature. We like to be beside the sea not because of the ice cream shops or the fun-fair rides or the Punch and Judy shows. It's because of the sea, the sand and the rocks: the elements of nature that resist man's tampering. Yes, we build our huts and sell cans of Coke and generally exploit the fact that there are large quantities of people here intent on enjoyment, but the main attraction is the sea, the water, the mysterious murk. We are drawn to the sea just as on holiday we may be drawn to horse riding, because in our everyday lives we have lost contact with nature. Instead we engage with representations of nature, mere images, whether in books, on television or on websites. Arthur, it seems, would rather spend time on a bird-watching website than look out of the window or—heaven forbid—go outside with his binoculars and look for birds in the hedges and fields where we live. Why? This must surely be the fault of his parents, this love of his for the easy cop-out of the computer and his problem with going outside. Yesterday we had to drag him—literally drag him—from the house for the one-mile meander down the hill and through the woods to our nearest beach. Once on the beach, though, he didn't want to leave.

Tether them no more, say Locke and Rousseau. Let them run free. Help: I am trying to let them run free but they are self-tethered to the computer. Arthur is staring at it now, as I write.

So, it is obvious that we yearn for nature, because we embrace it through the medium of holidays: at the beach or skiing. But here we have allowed our wild spirit and yearning for freedom to be commodified and exploited by the holiday industry. Would it not be better to weave nature into the fabric of your everyday life, rather than consign it to two costly weeks of freedom per year? Nature lives in your city garden. Get a plastic cup, half fill it with vodka, sink it in the flower bed and look at your catch after a few days. You'll be amazed at the number of beetles, spiders and weevils that are wandering around in your garden. Nature should not be separated into a "nature zone." Even in the deepest inner city, nature can be found on the doorstep. Just look at urban birds! They are not prejudiced against concrete. They nest on convenient spots and eat caterpillars and visit bird tables.

Don't waste money on expensive holidays. "It was awful," a friend told me yesterday of her $10,000 family trip to Tobago. "It rained every day, and there were four days of traveling." Everyone was thoroughly miserable. How much she would have preferred to have kept the money. It is low-cost, spontaneous, local trips that end up being more fun. You cannot plan your fun. You have to grab it as it passes, "kiss joy as it flies," as William Blake had it. Take trips. Stay with friends, of course. Split up. The nuclear family on holiday, four of you, each with completely different and probably violently opposing ideas of what constitutes "fun," is an absurd fantasy, a dream, a mere hope, sold to you as a reality by the peddlers of packaged products. For that $10,000 you could have bought a yurt for the garden or reduced your mortgage. And holidays are so horribly controlled: even as a child, I remember, I vaguely resented the overorganized nature of, for example, skiing trips—now there's a horrific waste of money if ever I saw one—as we poor consumers were herded from plane to bus to hotel with only a patronizing rep to negotiate between us and the outside world. Then it was mealtimes, lesson times and break times for a week. Like school. And after a week of this, it was back to school again, only the family was now considerably poorer and depressed by the return to grim, grinding reality. Yes, there had been a few moments of intense pleasure, skiing through woods; yes, there had at least been some sort of rupture in the quotidian routine, but was it worth the money? I would say not.

There exist much easier and cheaper ways to connect yourselves and your kids with nature. You need to disconnect yourself from the Matrix to discover them. I have already mentioned looking in the place too easily overlooked by most of us—directly under our own noses—but there is another trick, and that is camping. By camping I don't mean lugging the family down the motorway in a $30,000 plastic motor home in order to park on a character-free municipal lawn next to a trunk road with no view, with concrete toilet-block and SKY TV hookup. I took Arthur to one of these campsites near where I live, and I was shocked: what I saw were lonely families inside plastic huts watching television. It was a lovely sunny evening but no one was outside. Everyone was indoors, switched on and plugged in. It seems that "getting away from it all" has become "taking it all with you." I remember going on holiday to the Isle of Eigg. My friend DJ walked into the cabin where we were staying and looked at me pityingly: I had already plugged in my laptop. "What are you doing?" he demanded. "You're supposed to be getting away from all that shite." How right he was.

No, not that kind of camping. That's the kind of camping practiced by people who lack the freedom gene. Again, we need to exercise our own imaginations rather than just automatically reaching for the mouse when a decision is to be made. We idle parents want to sit round the campfire and drink beer and sing songs while our children play. Think of the great wandering artist Augustus John roaming the countryside with his wives and children and caravan. It's decommodified camping that we want. Find a friend with a field, get a bunch of friends or four other families and camp up for the weekend. Why not rent or buy a field with some friends so you have your own wild camping spot? Instead of the two-week family holiday, organize little trips all throughout the summer.

Last year we had great success with this approach and were lucky enough to be invited by friends who had access to some land for two or three such weekends. There were ten adults and about twenty children—no tellies, no computers—and the kids played among themselves and left us alone. I woke up every morning in the tent surrounded by empty beds. The kids had already got themselves up and were inventing games in the woods. We did not need to make any effort to "entertain" them. They entertained themselves, while we adults got on with the important business of making tea, talking and nursing our hangovers. If you can't find a field, it's possible to find wilder campsites, the sort where you can camp next to a stream and light fires. It's cheap and easy, a return to nature's never-disappointing bounty, where sticks and stones are toys. Or just camp in someone else's garden, or even in your own.

And in addition to frequent camping trips, you can weave the fabric of nature into everyday life. Even in homes without gardens, you can grow flowers and vegetables in pots and trays. Or get a plot and make it into your own fruit-and-veg paradise, with dens and sheds. Kids love sowing seeds and watching them grow, and there is no tastier treat than peas eaten straight from the pod. Let nature do the work.

Blackberry picking is a great activity. Brambles grow everywhere, and our family trips when I was young to a nearby wasteland to gather blackberries stand out in my memory with far greater intensity than listless mornings spent watching kids' TV. And blackberry picking leads to the practical benefits of blackberry crumble and blackberry jam. Hunt for food in the hedgerows, get hold of Richard Mabey's *Food for Free* and go foraging.

Streams, rivers, pebbles, rocks . . . this was the message of Wordsworth: nature will unite what man has rent asunder. It is a harmonizer, whereas the ice cream shop creates rifts and enmities. For me, one of the greatest nature philosophers of recent times is Masanobu Fukuoka, author of *The One-Straw Revolution*, published in 1978. This remarkable book was written after Fukuoka had spent twenty years on his small farm perfecting what he called "do-nothing farming." The Oriental concept of "do nothing" is close to my own idea of idleness. It does not refer to goofing off or giving up, but rather to letting go, going with the flow, a wise and merry detachment. It is, in Aldous Huxley's phrase, an "active resignation." So when Fukuoka talks about "do-nothing farming," he does not mean that he sits around doing nothing while everything around him turns into a wilderness. What he means is that he creates situations where nature will do the work with minimum interference from man. Therefore he does not plow or add chemical fertilizers to the crops. Instead he simply puts the rice straw back on the ground after harvesting and scatters chicken manure on it. At other times he sows clover, which works as a green manure. That's about it, but he says that with these techniques he can equal the yield of fields farmed with modern methods:

> I have demonstrated in my fields that natural farming produces harvests comparable to those of modern scientific agriculture. If the results of a non-active agriculture are comparable to those of science, at a fraction of the investment in labor and resources, then where is the benefit of scientific technology?

In the same way, Fukuoka says, we should let children grow up on their own, and refrain from our high-energy, high-impact, hard-work meddling, our high-intensity child-rearing techniques, constantly requiring toil and money. We need low-impact parenting, do-nothing parenting, no-work parenting. Harness natural processes, and nature will do the work for you. In the case of gardening, this may involve a lot of simply wandering about. Just sitting in your garden or strolling around it will produce umpteen ideas for low-effort improvement and refinement. So it is with children. Just sit near them with a book and watch them play and chatter. Here is some choice wisdom from Fukuoka, recommending we leave well alone:

> From the time they enter nursery school, people's sorrows begin. The human being was a happy creature, but he created a hard world and now struggles to break out of it.
>
> In nature there is life and death, and nature is joyful. In human society there is life and death, and people live in sorrow.

The scientists who rejoiced when rocks were brought back from the moon have less grasp of the moon than the children who sing out, "How old are you, Mr. Moon?" The poet Basho could apprehend the wonder of nature by watching the reflection of the full moon in the tranquillity of a pond. All the scientists did when they went off into space and stomped around in their space boots was to tarnish a bit of the moon's splendor for millions of lovers and children on the earth.

In a similar spirit, we must stop interfering with the lives of our children. This does not mean abandonment, any more than natural farming means that you let the brambles take over. Neither does it mean that you don't think about what you are doing and take responsibility for it. You also need to provide good soil for the kids to grow in, for your little seedlings. The plethora of consumer objects and the nonstop advertising that pushes them on children is a commercial form of interfering. Consumer objects are like chemical fertilizer: they seem like a good idea at the time, but as each year passes more and more are needed. And children become reliant on them. All are diversions from the natural life of the spirit, which can actually rediscover itself on rocky shores, by the sea, in meadows or woodlands, in the wild places or even in the cracks between paving stones.

Rousseau talks about "natural" childhood, and Fukuoka talks about "natural" farming. The message is the same: Leave them alone. Trust them. Provide fertile conditions and they will grow. Create sturdy, strong seedlings. The idle parent would like to see his children thrive in groups, growing up strong and sturdy amongst the weeds, rather than hothoused and intensively cultivated.

Natural parenting is gentle and easy. It requires very little work and should produce strong, healthy, unique, confident children. It is not about imposing an ideology on the kids or about creating an "ideal" adult. It is about letting them grow up in all their unique individuality, growing into who they are. Like zucchini seeds: we carefully place them in a pot of high-quality compost before planting the seedlings outside when they have grown; we have gradually accustomed it to life outdoors.

And even more important than giving nature to our kids is learning what nature is from our kids. As Fukuoka argues: "That which is conceived to be nature is only the *idea* of nature arising in each person's mind. The ones who see true nature are infants. They see without thinking, straight and clear."

But all too soon we move infants from this nondiscriminating natural apprehension of the world to one which is mediated through books, teachers and websites: so, as I have remarked, Arthur would rather watch birds on a screen than stare out of the

window at the bird feeder with its huge and busy crowd of chicka-
dees. Why? This is what we have taught him. Having said this,
Arthur has just now come in and asked for a matchbox. He had a
beetle in his hand and wanted to put it somewhere. So perhaps we
need not fret too much.

But yes, we can learn from small children a nonjudgmental
acceptance of the ways of the world. A little child sits in the middle of a field and plays with the grass. He doesn't think, "How
beautiful this is! What a lovely day! Not a cloud in the sky!" These
are all man-made ideas. The little child just is. Not an idea in his
head, no bookish notions, prejudices, morals, resolutions, self-
reflective agonies, needs to escape, doubts, fears. He doesn't even
look or examine. He does not watch a sunset—to watch something
is to remove yourself from it. He *is* the sunset. But pretty soon we
leave this Garden of Eden. Self-consciousness, pain and fig leaves
come between us and the natural world, and we spend the whole
of the rest of our lives trying to get back in.

5.

The More, the Merrier

Utere convivis, non tristibus utere amicis, quos nugae et risus,
et joca salsa juvant.
(Feast often, and use friends not still so sad,
whose jests and merriments may make thee glad.)
ROBERT BURTON, *The Anatomy of Melancholy*, 1621

Packed with wisdom though they are, there is something that niggles about both Rousseau's *Émile* and Locke's *Some Thoughts Concerning Education*, and it is this: their charges appear to be friendless. The child is isolated. While both stress the importance of play and pleasure in the child's life, and are filled with generous ideas about education and nature, this is a world apart from the medieval scene, where life was lived collectively. Just look at Pieter Bruegel's painting *Children's Games*, where 250 children play together, without a parent in sight. But Rousseau's Émile and Locke's imaginary pupil are kept away from the rough boys. This shift from a messy, sociable conviviality to a hothouse isolation reflects, of course, the big historic shift that happened somewhere between 1400 and 1600, that is, the isolation of the individual. We compare Pieter Bruegel's painting *Children's Games* (1560), which, with great technical skill, shows 250 children playing, with the formal portraits of Joshua Reynolds, which show melancholy posh kids, alone and dressed up. While medieval cathedrals, for example, burst with life at every corner, art after the Renaissance tends to present man as a lonely individual: the use of perspective (as well as lenses, according to David Hockney in *Secret Knowledge*) isolates man in time and space.

The problem with Locke and Rousseau is that they are concerned with molding. This was very much a Puritan idea in education: that the child could and should be molded in order to function effectively in a certain sort of society. And although Locke and Rousseau's molding is of the most kind and liberal sort, it is still a form of molding; and in order to be molded, the child needs to be separated from other people. For the idle parent, this sounds far too much like hard work and we question, anyway, whether it's good for the kid.

It's a theme that we find explored in journalist Barbara Ehrenreich's book *Dancing in the Streets: A History of Collective Joy*. She argues that an "epidemic of melancholy" started around 1600, around the time when Robert Burton began work on *The Anatomy of Melancholy*. Burton wrote that melancholy produces "a cankered soul macerated with cares and discontents, a being tired of life . . . [who] cannot endure company, light, or life itself." Ehrenreich quotes the historian Lionel Trilling, who wrote: "In the late sixteenth and early seventeenth centuries, something like a mutation in human nature took place." The historian Yi-Fu Tuan, she says, describes a new "isolation, loneliness, a sense of disengagement, a loss of natural vitality and of innocent pleasure in the givenness of the world." Ehrenreich argues that this new kind of isolated individual does not find freedom but on the contrary suffers from a kind of dependency, a dependency on how they are seen by the outside world: "How am I doing?" is the question that the new isolated self asks. With the loss of the medieval sense of community comes a new seriousness.

When I interviewed Barbara Ehrenreich recently, I brought up the issue of the loneliness of the modern family. I mentioned to her the example of Alia Hartman, a Mexican journalist now living in Germany with her German husband. "Life is so much harder here," Hartman said to me, at a conference on laziness. "In Mexico there are lots of people to help, aunts, uncles, friends. In Germany you are on your own." Ehrenreich, now a grandmother, contrasted her grandchildren's style of life with that of her own kids:

> The kids don't just run from house to house the way my daughter did when she was growing up. Our backyards were not separated and the kids would all be out in a common space. It's so much more controlled now. But kids like nothing better than to run in packs. They love that ebb and flow.

So this is the flaw in Locke and Rousseau: the isolation. Having isolated our adult selves, we now isolate children. I hear that in New York sleepovers are virtually unknown, so rampant has fear of the pedophilia become. Sleepovers have always seemed to me to be an excellent idea for the idle parent, either way around: if your kid is off staying with a friend, that's a blessed break for you. If your kid has a friend to stay, then they will amuse themselves, meaning that you can get on with the important things, like weeding, drinking beer, practicing the ukulele or staring out of the window.

The whole purpose of this book is to encourage you to resist the work-hard-in-isolation Puritan culture and its inventions, such as school and the full-time job, and bring back some good, old-fashioned conviviality and providential thinking, in childhood as well as adulthood. And this is why friends are so important: put simply, they make life easier.

In Aldous Huxley's utopian novel *Island*, the hero finds himself stranded on an island called Pala, where the inhabitants have created a society that harmonizes the best of Western science with the best of Eastern mysticism. Now, their solution to the problem of the confining nuclear family is precisely to spread the burden, and they do this by means of Mutual Adoption Clubs. The idea is that each family connects itself to a network of twenty or so other families. At any time a child from one can go and stay with the family of another. This system provides an escape valve from the confinement of the nuclear family. As Sulina, a Palanese mother, explains:

Escape is built into the new system. Whenever the parental Home Sweet Home becomes too unbearable, the child is allowed, is actively encouraged—and the whole weight of public opinion is behind the encouragement—to migrate to one of its other homes. We all have our quota of deputy mothers, deputy fathers, deputy aunts and uncles, deputy babies and toddlers and teenagers.

It's an idea we could take up immediately. By extending the family, creating a network of mutually supporting friends and neighbors, in short, by helping each other, family life could be made very much easier.

But we are fearful today. When I was growing up in the 1970s, we would leave the house in the morning, get on our bicycles and play all day in the streets. Or go into the woods. When I was four I took my two-year-old brother two blocks up the road, on our own, to find the ice cream lady. Children should be running around in packs, but instead they are shut in their bedroom with only a big TV and computer games for company. "I know he's safe in there," a mother chillingly told the cameras on a recent television show about modern childhood. Clearly this isolation also suits the consumer culture: alone and staring at a screen, the child is easy prey for advertisers. Playing in a field with friends, he is not playing his part in the economy.

Arthur comes home from school and goes straight on to a website called Club Penguin, where, he says, he can "talk" to his friend Sam. Call me a Luddite—and I love the Luddites, by the way—but surely it would be cheaper, easier and healthier to have Sam visit in person?

The simple antidote to isolation is more friends, more fun, more festivity. I have noticed that the larger the group of kids, the easier life becomes for the parents. They don't bother you. One child alone will say, "I'm bored." "Go outside." "But there's nothing to do outside." "Play in the tree house. Or how about some drawing?" "Awwwww, I DON'T WANT TO." At this point the parent may well lose his temper—justifiably so. A whining, dependent child is annoying. The only thing that will satisfy this bored child is a one-on-one game of Monopoly. But I don't want to play Monopoly with a seven-year-old. I want to go and read in the garden and smoke a roll-up. However, if there are two kids playing together, things improve. A little bit of bothering, but not so much. And as soon as there are three or more they practically vanish into thin air, and that's precisely what we're after. You leave them alone, and even better, they leave you alone. Hodgkinson's Law: The more, the merrier. Many hands make light work, and many kids make the parent's work lighter. Added to this is the real pleasure of seeing them play happily. In the distance.

We recently achieved a Bruegel-type situation at our annual village medieval banquet. While the adults ate and drank, a huge gang of children played games of their own making in the field next to the tent. That, I repeat, is my idea of child care: a beer tent next to a playing field or wood. Parents in one, kids in the other. There's nothing worse at festivals than "kids' zones." Go into a kids' zone (the kids are not allowed in them unsupervised, which wrecks the purpose of them, as far as I can tell) and you will see bored parents weakly smiling as their children try and fail to juggle neon balls. It's hell on earth. Almost as bad as the playground. Swings! Kill me, quickly, before I die of boredom.

All you need is a field. Just one field. No swings or climbing frames. Parents and beer at one end, kids playing all over it.

At a festival last year Arthur made friends with the boys from the family camping next door. Every morning he would disappear off with them and play all day. We discovered from their lovely mother that they lived in a community, a commune. Arthur discovered this, too, but put it in slightly different terms: "Billy lives with his friends!" he told me, as if this was one of the most fantastic things he could think of—to live with your friends!

Sadness in adults can be caused by a sense of isolation, and it is to be cured not by Prozac but by conviviality. It is worth asking whether the same is true of children. Perhaps we just need to get them singing and dancing.

One key difference between medieval notions of childhood and modern approaches is in the nature/nurture debate. In the twelfth and thirteenth centuries, it was believed that if a boy of noble birth was brought up by peasants then, sooner or later, his noble nature would emerge. Nature was all. I like that idea. It lets the parents off the hook. You don't really matter. You submit to God's will. That actually relieves the burden on parents. However, by the time of Locke, man's input has become the crucial factor: "of all the men we meet with, nine parts of ten are what they are, good or evil, useful or not, by their education." This view persists today: the psychologist Oliver James, for example, is firmly of the view that parenting is everything, that the atmosphere in the home, particularly in your early years, is the key element in determining your character. In Locke we see the new importance of education. And parents. If kids can be nine-tenths molded, then it would be irresponsible of the parents to let go of the responsibility for the molding. Therefore since we are unlikely ever to reach a scientific conclusion in the debate—because we will never, ever, know the answer—I propose that each of us simply invent a nature/nurture theory that suits us and then go out and find evidence for that theory, which, after all, is the common method among historians and scientists, whatever they may try to tell you about objectivity.

The idle parent, I think, would probably like to settle on a split of one-third nature, two-thirds nurture. That would mean that we are not entirely without importance in a child's life, but that most of it is up to them. I think that would give them due respect, too, and in general we don't give our kids enough respect. Sorry to repeat, but it's worth repeating: we are always interfering, whether by organizing ceaseless activities or telling them off or sitting down with them for—and this may be worse—a "serious chat" (horror of all horrors), an attempt to feel their pain and really care, to become all dewy-eyed and sympathetic. This attempt at empathy is itself a kind of intrusion or interference, a presumption. How can we possibly get inside somebody else's head, least of all a child's? I remember the pain and agony when my dad would sit down with me for a heart-to-heart. My dad was doing his best, being good, in fact, but maybe it's not required. Certainly I can see this with Arthur if I try to give him a stern-but-fair-and-loving chat—he writhes and squirms and says anything to bring the experience to a swift conclusion.

So if you want to make life easy for yourself and fun for your kids, you must organize things so that they are in large groups as much as possible. Don't coop them up in cars, in the nuclear household, in front of a screen. And in your own household, why separate them into individual bedrooms? We found that our children wanted to be together, like a pile of hamsters. So now they all sleep in the same room. First Arthur asked to be with Henry. And then daughter Delilah said she was lonely in her bedroom alone. So now, although they fight, I think they are happier.

And that brings me to another point: adult friends. We like to sit drinking in the kitchen with our adult guests while the kids run wild around the house or in the garden, doing whatever they like doing.

That was the great revelation that came after we moved to the country. Instead of shuffling the children off to bed and holding a stressful dinner party, we find that families locally get together for a late lunch at weekends. Piles of adults everywhere and piles of kids everywhere. And I, who had been missing my late-night drinking sessions, found a solution: start drinking earlier! By the time nine o'clock came round I was ready for bed. But I'd had a great time drinking beer all afternoon. With other adults. While the kids looked after themselves. This is the way of societies that are less industrialized than ours: people, people, everywhere! Conviviality and merriment, these are the keys.

It's also true to say that a little bit of booze weakens the authoritative dad. You become less strict: "Of course you can eat that huge pile of Gummi Bears! Eat away! What do I care?" It is astonishing what a relief it is to stop trying to be an authority figure and instead be a partner to your kids. Be imperfect, let go. My friend Kate told me what a relief it was when she stopped hassling her teenage son about smoking and just let him do it (an approach recommended by Summerhill School founder A. S. Neill, by the way). Give them respect and let them do what they want. This is not, incidentally, the same thing as license. You do not allow them to smash up the car, spit at people, hit them. No. But you can be strict and free at the same time.

When we live in a large group of people, we are given a glimpse of what living without authority feels like, of living in a self-governed, self-determined way. No longer the tin-pot dictator in the home, flailing around, trying and failing to instill discipline, shouting and raving and slamming doors. We become, when tipsy, detached, amused, an equal with the children. They are running about in a gang doing whatever they want, and we are running about in a gang doing whatever we want. For a short time, before we return to the everyday tyranny of the family, we are living in a tribe, with no bosses, no timetables, no buses, no money to be earned or tax returns to be filed.

This weekend we held a big party for eighty or so friends and neighbors and their kids. It was a huge pleasure to see the boys dashing here and there, all different heights. There was no whining or pleading, just unsupervised play all day long. Yes, there were one or two bleeding noses and a bit of rubbish to clear up, but the day was more or less harmonious. Yes, they left their sweaters lying everywhere, but they are children and cannot be expected to think of others in an adult way. A. S. Neill wrote that he picked up piles of sweaters from around the grounds of Summerhill every day. However many times you tell them to pick up after themselves, they will not do it. So don't bother. Let that one go. Accept that you are going to be picking up sweaters. It's not really that bad.

Kids belong to a different species. We can respect their ways, but we cannot get into their heads. And every time we think we have come close we find that they have changed, grown out of that phase. The sentence "It's just a phase" is a great friend to the idle parent, and it is often true. You start worrying about some particular aspect of their behavior—clinginess, for example—only to find that while you were worrying they have grown out of it. So why bother worrying? As A. S. Neill writes: "By nature he is self-interested and he seeks always to try his power." Children are selfish, but they grow out of it.

6.

Down with School

How can happiness be bestowed? My own answer is:
Abolish authority. Let the child be himself. Don't push him around.
Don't teach him. Don't lecture him. Don't elevate him.

Don't force him to do anything.

A. S. NEILL, *Summerhill*, 1960

Teach the three R's and leave the children to look out
for their own aims. . . . Who has wit and guts doesn't starve:
neither does he care about starving.

D. H. LAWRENCE, "Education of the People"

Education is a servant to the economy. Education is now
thoroughly subordinated to the supposed inevitabilities of
globalization and international economic competition.

STEPHEN J. BALL, *The Education Debate*, 2008

We start this chapter with a paradoxical idea, that in order to best educate your child you must give him as little education as possible. There is far too much organized, formal education in the world—education meaning moral brainwashing, free babysitting, academies of stupidity, schools, which in the words of The Clash "teach you how to be thick." John Lennon, too, was antischool; just recall the lyrics of "Working Class Hero." It's worth remembering that the explosion of grammar schools in the sixteenth and seventeenth centuries was motivated by the Protestant notion that you could mold children to be faithful servants of the economy and of God. In contrast to the medieval system, which admitted a huge variety of approaches to life, including beggary and idleness, after the Reformation human existence began to be standardized, idealized. Contemplation was out and hard work was in. An abstract idea of perfection began to enter the culture, and the idea that man was put on this earth to work at perfecting himself. Those who promoted the idea of education tended to argue that it improved the general level of morality: that kids could reform parents. One Bishop White Kennett wrote in a 1706 publication titled *The Charity of Schools for Poor Children*:

> Some parents have been regenerated and born anew by the influence of their own flesh and blood. To see the children between the school hours delighting in their books and lessons at home, this by degree has turned the hearts of the par-

ents the same way; they have recovered their lost reading and have been restored to the knowledge and practice of morality and religion.

A similar point was made by the Protestant philosopher Richard Baxter in 1673: "By all means let children be taught to read . . . or else you deprive them of a singular help to their instruction and salvation."

It was felt also among Protestant educators that if people were taught how to read then it would be easier to control the ideas they were exposed to. Books could be chosen for the people in a way that preachers could not. In this way salvation changed from a public spectacle—medieval churchgoers would stream from the churches in floods of tears—to a matter of private study. Another educational writer made the point that "misorders" and "disobedience" could be avoided in young people if they were taught to read.

Here we see the ideological foundations of the school system that still exists today: education as moral instruction, and reading valued insofar as it makes brainwashing easier and helps the individual to play their part in the commercial world. Today teachers' moans tend to be of two sorts: they complain about the bureaucracy and centralization of education, the iron control imposed by central government, but they also complain that they are merely preparing children for the job market, turning out obedient little worker bees ready to be enslaved by the corporations and thinking it is freedom.

So history gives us a confusing picture. Education is seen by some as a route to liberty and by others as a means of brainwashing.

It is the object of the idle educator to turn out children with wit and guts, as D. H. Lawrence put it. It is also the role of the idle educator to ensure that children are enjoying themselves right here and right now, in the present. Practically every modern book I read about child care, however liberal and well intentioned its ideas might be, talks about "investing in the future"; I would prefer to read about "contemplating the present." We still persist in believing that the present is not really very important and it is the future that we should be interested in. That word "invest" fills me with horror too: as if children are little capitalistic enterprises that we must invest in now in order to get some sort of return in the future. The word "investment" turns children into the objects of greed. The whole idea of the "future" is a capitalist concept, whose religious counterpart is in the Protestant idea of "salvation." No, we must work to ensure that every moment of every day is intense and filled with pleasure, joy, fun, laughter and passion.

For D. H. Lawrence, education should be a simple matter of teaching children to read and write and any kind of moral instruction should be avoided altogether.

If we were content to teach a child to read and write and do his modicum of arithmetic, just as at an earlier stage his mother teaches him to walk and to talk, so that he may toddle his little way upon the face of the earth by himself, it would be all right. It would be a thousand times better, as things stand, to chuck overboard all your drawing and painting and music and modeling and pseudo-science and "graphic" history and "graphic" geography and "self-expression," all the lot. Pitch them overboard, teach the three R's, and then proceed with a certain amount of technical instruction, in preparation for the coming job. For all the rest, for all that concerns the child himself, leave him alone.

Today in schools, much emphasis is put on moral instruction from a very young age indeed. In typically arid fashion, children are given targets for ethical achievements. On a hideously overdesigned school report for Delilah, who is six, there are the following check boxes:

6. Understand that there need to be agreed values and codes of behavior for groups of people, including adults and children, to work together harmoniously.
7. Understand that people have different needs, views, cultures and beliefs that need to be treated with respect.
8. Understand that s/he can expect others to treat her or his needs, views, cultures and beliefs with respect.

These are just three of 120 such achievements to be ticked off. (And are not point 6 and point 7 mutually incompatible?)

Well, I won't go on, but really. What a load of poppycock. "Joshua, I really respect your views regarding that toy that you have just snatched from me, and I respect that you have a different view as to its current ownership. But I really do think that you need to respect my belief that the toy should now be in my possession." I've noticed that kids use adult morals for their own ends: "Share, share!" they screech when attempting to take a toy from another child.

This idea of her "cultures and beliefs" is repeated again and again in the report. Six-year-olds don't have cultures and beliefs, do they? It's absurd. I also object to the training in computers: six-year-olds should apparently find out "about and identify the uses of technology and uses of information and communication technology and programmable toys to support his/her learning." What if the parents have a culture that has decided to throw the computer and programmable toys out of the window? What then?

We may agree with some of these ethical precepts or we may not. The real point is that the state is interfering to such a degree in the first place, in trying to mold the ethics of a whole nation. The state! Which itself is entirely free of morals and is built on the self-interest of an oligarchy. Why should it tell our children how to behave?

Bertrand Russell tells us that state-run education is a recent phenomenon:

> The interest of the State in education is very recent. It did not exist in antiquity or the Middle Ages; until the Renaissance, education was only valued by the Church. The Renaissance brought an interest in advanced scholarship. . . . The Reformation, in England and Germany, brought a desire on the part of the

State to have some control over universities and grammar schools, to prevent them from remaining hotbeds of "Popery." But this interest soon evaporated.

We must resist state control. Elsewhere we find the sinister word "appropriate" being used when discussing, really meaning "in such a way as we approve of." As Bertrand Russell pointed out about the famous headmaster Dr. Arnold, "moral evil" meant whatever he wanted to change in his boys. Morality is a relative concept and should not be state-controlled.

School days are too long. Lawrence recommends three hours a day of intellectual pursuits, with one hour for "physical and domestic training." This idea would fit in with the idle parent's working day: three or four hours and that's it. The rest of the day can be spent lying around in the sun reading (you) and playing somewhere in the distance without you (them). Both you and they should also spend time learning plumbing, carpentry, gardening, painting: skills that will make of your children proud, capable and independent individuals.

While school has a superficial attraction to the idle parent as a free babysitting service, giving you peace during the day, the idle parent will in fact have to take on much responsibility for their child's education.

So, what are the alternatives? Well, some of you will go the whole way and embrace homeschooling, a wonderful option. The organization Education Otherwise exists to help parents who want to go down this route, and certainly some of the testimonials from parents make inspiring reading:

Having children who love to learn and are always busy making, doing and discovering has made autonomous education easy. On a sunny day any number of learning experiences happen in a few hours. Someone makes a sign to warn others of a slippery path using wood, nails and paint. Others run in and out to identify a butterfly or plant; someone else picks fruit and divides it equally for lunch; another makes cheese on toast; dens are built; complex chasing or role play games go on; tree climbing, dam building, birdwatching, leaf printing, water play and so on. Inside it is just the same only lots of paper, pens, glue, Lego, soft toys, blocks, ramps are involved and I'm often presented with a map of an island or clues for a treasure hunt (for an apple!) or a poem or a radio program someone taped and wanted to share. . . . My role as "teacher" seems much more to listen to what they have learned themselves than ever to "teach" them anything. Apart from learning to read and a few other basics, most of what they know comes from reading, discussing and discovering for themselves.

The primary objection to homeschooling, always made by dullards who have not thought the matter through, is that "school provides social life." The home educators fight back with the convincing argument that the social life they get at school is not necessarily a healthy one: "The social life of most schools and classrooms is mean-spirited, status-oriented, competitive and snobbish." They also point out that it's easy for parents to organize a social life for the kids: friends come and play, learning groups are formed with other home educators in the area, and there are umpteen sport, outdoor and drama classes available. They point out that these out-of-school relationships are based on common interest and emerge from choice rather than necessity.

Homeschooling, though, may seem daunting. Certainly the experiences that Victoria and I have had trying to teach Arthur have not been particularly successful. He seems much happier at school. Perhaps we are lucky with our school, as our kids attend a small rural primary school with only about forty kids, aged from five to eleven. We love the school, but we do a lot of reading and talking with the kids outside school. I also teach ukulele there, and Victoria has helped with the drama group. It's easy to get involved with primary schools; they appreciate the extra input, as they are more used to parents moaning.

The most important factor in all this is probably parents' own mental attitude. If you have respect for your child, if you are not trying to mold the child into some perfect ideal, then all options are valid. We are not talking about a glib list of rules for you to apply in order to make your children happy.

In fact, we're not even aiming for happiness; we are aiming for strength, freedom and joy in our children and in ourselves. We're aiming for satisfaction. Even awareness of the limitation of school as a place for education may itself be enough to liberate your kids.

We need to abandon the quest for perfection and even the need for authority. Neill warns: "The adult has striven for perfection in his own life, has failed miserably to reach it, and now attempts to find it in his children."

This danger is just as real for supposedly enlightened parents as for traditional ones. And this is perhaps another problem with

Locke and Rousseau. Although their ideas on freedom and wildness are certainly to be applauded, and there is much inspiring
material in their books, they can tend to make us feel failures because as imperfect people we will inevitably fail to implement
their ideal schemes. Idealism can in fact be a sort of tyranny:
many are the times in my own home when I have been accused by
Victoria of being a bully and a tyrant, for example, when I have
unplugged the television mid-show. You can't impose freedom by
authority. The other day Delilah and I were dancing to a CD in the
kitchen. Arthur came in and pulled the plug out.

"What the hell are you doing?" I asked. "Why are you spoiling
our fun?"

"Well, you spoil our fun when you turn the telly off."

"Erm . . . that's different," I spluttered.

So the idealist can become a bully. Better to lead by example
or not lead at all. Get on with your own life and allow others to get
on with theirs. William Blake warns against an excess of thou-
shalt-not-ism in "The Garden of Love":

> I went to the Garden of Love,
> And saw what I had never seen;
> A Chapel was built in the midst,
> Where I used to play on the green.
>
> And the gates of this Chapel were shut
> And "Thou shalt not," writ over the door;
> So I turned to the Garden of Love
> That so many sweet flowers bore.

And I saw it was filled with graves,
And tombstones where flowers should be;
And priests in black gowns were walking their rounds,
And binding with briars my joys and desires.

Send your children to school with some jokes that they can tell. Or a magic trick to perform. What kind of school might look attractive to the idle parent? England has the liberated Summerhill School, founded by the previously mentioned A. S. Neill, whose book I would recommend to all parents, whether or not they send their kid or kids to his school. Summerhill is a boarding school that practices self-government. This means that the children themselves are involved in the running of the school. They vote on rules and they go only to the lessons they choose to. The authority element is removed. By these means, Neill argues, much time is saved: when children have chosen to learn, they learn at a far faster rate than when the learning has been imposed on them by an outside authority. At Summerhill kids might barely go to lessons for three years, but they will then suddenly work very hard when they realize that they need math credits, for example, if they want to go to art school.

The nice thing about private education is that it is not run by the state. Everyone who is there has chosen to be there. This immediately gives a self-governed feeling of independence to the school. Many private schools are curiously much closer to the anarchist idea of what a school should look like than state-run schools. Recently, a former Eton schoolmaster wrote an article praising the system and the attitudes at the school in an anarchist magazine called *Total Liberty*:

> If schooling is the regimented, hierarchical, disciplined, closing down of young people, then education is the free cooperative opening up of young people. . . . Education is the facilitation of environments where people can develop their own interests, can learn to be autonomous individuals, and have the space and opportunity to interact in groups characterized by flat, open forms of organization. In schools like Eton, there exists an active culture, driven by the young people, which can be seen to match this paradigm.

He argues that this way the elite are given the education to be free while the rest of us are tied down to target-driven government ideologies. He goes on to talk about the huge number of societies run by the boys, for example, the Orwell Society:

> These young men were absolutely dedicated to the anti-war campaign, and organized an endless stream of events to support the anti-war movement. They attended all the London demonstrations, they handed out leaflets in the local towns, and they campaigned within the school. Interestingly, the government's attitude to state-school pupils being involved in much of the anti-war activity was that any absences would be treated as "truancy," and punished. The members of the Orwell Society spoke to the Head Master, and convinced him that their involvement was necessary and that it was right. His response was to accept these arguments.

. . .

Certainly I've noticed that boys who went to Eton have an enviable degree of self-assurance, whatever their chosen path through life. And that is good. The idle parent wants strong, resilient, bright-eyed, fearless children. We want confidence and courage. Remember also that Eton gave us George Orwell and Aldous Huxley, the two great prophets of the twentieth century.

The author of the piece also mentions the short hours at Eton: "Etonians were always horrified to learn that the school day for most pupils in the UK is from [8:45 to 3:30], without interruption. Etonians spend only half a day in the classroom each day." Which itself would tend to prove that paradox stated at the beginning of this chapter: less is more. At my own school, Westminster, the school terms were at least two weeks shorter than state-school terms, but the exam results were infinitely better. Also, we enjoyed ourselves. There was a huge degree of freedom, and I think it was a result of the attitudes of the teachers to the pupils and vice versa. That attitude can be summed up in the phrase mutual respect.

We also had the most fantastic teachers, such as Richard Jacobs, who taught us English. Sometimes he would spend the entire lesson talking about red wine, and he'd hold tastings in his flat. Other times he would take us to stare at the Rothkos in the Tate Gallery for half an hour. Once he gave us a free lesson because he said he was going to find it "too painful" to read over with us the scene in *Othello* where he throws money at Desdemona. That was one of the best lessons I ever had. He would also tell us about his nights out at Heaven, the gay nightclub. He never had any problem with discipline for the simple reason that he never tried to impose authority. One day he came in and said, bemoaning his lack of literary achievements: "I'm twenty-five today. Keats *died* at twenty-five!" He also taught us about Roland Barthes and the post-structuralists, and introduced us to poets like Geoffrey Hill. He taught us about Piero della Francesca and the *Annunciation*. None of this stuff was anywhere near the syllabus, I might add. All these stories and more have remained firmly lodged in my mind. He brought pleasure and intensity to learning.

Yes, I know. I can hear programmed liberal voice complaining that not everybody can afford private school. What I am trying to do is open your minds to other possibilities. And certainly not everybody at Westminster was exactly rich in my day: the parents were doctors, journalists, architects, actors, writers. They were working professionals rather than filthy-rich city types or aristocrats.

Think about your priorities. Eve Libertine of the punk band Crass wanted to send her son Nemo to Summerhill. But she had no money. So she lived frugally—in a shared house—and ran a market stall at the weekends. With the profits of her stall, she was able to pay Nemo's fees. People today spend money on cars, holidays, enormous televisions, usury charges and mobile phones but will not spend a single penny on their own children's education. Most families could save nearly $17,000 a year by cutting out all such luxuries. Think about your priorities. Most of those rich people you see are not really rich. They are merely massively in debt. They have chosen to shoulder a debt in order to pay for things like school fees. What I'm saying is: Don't complain. Just live.

What really is astonishing is when the upper middle classes, people who in every other respect elevate themselves above others by their spending habits, suddenly come over all socialist when it comes to their own child's education. They go out for meals in restaurants twice a week and take taxis, they take on big houses with big mortgages, but they complain about the unfairness of private schools. This is the beauty of taking an anarchist position: it frees you to do what you want, private school, state school or some kind of home-based system.

Another answer is to make your local school more like Eton. Encourage your kids to start societies and to question the authorities at their school. Take them off a week early. Take Fridays off and go camping. We often take the kids off on a Friday or a Monday.

I would like to see a total destruction of the educational system as it stands, and for it to be replaced with a chaotic free-for-all, where individual teachers can advertise their services, where schools could consist of three kids or a thousand, where parents would get together and hire a tutor for their children.

Our local primary school is good because of the teachers, who do their job in spite of, not helped by, the state with its absurd panoply of check boxes and test-score targets, which have nothing to do with the real purpose of education. State education means a poor education for everyone and an education that is centrally controlled and operated by the state. And as the group of people who operate the state is constantly changing, so teachers have to put up with new approaches and new ideologies every couple of years. The problem here is not whether or not we agree with the ideology—certain elements we will, others not. The point is that ideologies themselves are by nature totalitarian.

One option that has not been well explored would be some kind of community school. A group of local families could get together and pay one or two teachers to teach their kids. This approach would be far cheaper than private school. I imagine four hours each morning of hard work, followed by outdoor activities. My ideal term would be just eleven weeks long. But the real advantage of community schools is that each would be different, each would be uniquely adapted to its own distinctive area and its own distinctive group of pupils and parents. One of my main objections to state schooling is the stifling uniformity that it places on diverse people. This crushing of individuality has led to an outbreak of schoolyard massacres in the United States, like Columbine, for example. Let that be a lesson to us.

Our community school could be a wonderful place. Employ a bright young man fresh out of university to teach your kids in the morning. Imagine being Wordsworth and Dorothy and Southey in the Lake District, with the young Mr. De Quincey teaching English in their little self-administered school. In the days of Locke (himself educated at Westminster) and Rousseau, it was taken as understood that the middle-class family would have a tutor. Locke argues that it is better to give up purposeless luxuries and spend money on education: "Spare it in toys and play-games, in silk and ribbons, laces and other useless expenses, as much as you please;

but be not sparing in so necessary a part as this. 'Tis not good husbandry to make his fortune rich and his mind poor."

Locke devotes several pages to advice on how a tutor should be selected. Let's imagine that you have found a tutor. And you are going to help with your little school yourself. As are other parents. You have three eleven-week terms, each with a week's holiday in the middle. That's 150 days of school each year. If the tutor is to teach four hours a day, then you will have to pay him or her for 600 hours. Let's pay him well and give him about $33 an hour. So that adds up to $20,000 a year. Between, say, four families with two kids, that's $5,000 per year, or just $2,500 per child. When you consider that some families spend $15,000 a year or more on nurseries and child care, and when you consider the enormous expense of private schools (which can now only be afforded by the most avaricious of hedge-fund managers) then $2,500 seems a relatively trifling expense, to have your own community school with your own teachers of your own selection.

Imagine how quickly your children would learn and how much time they would have for mucking about. The teaching itself would be more intense, leaving more time for fooling, more fun. More trips, more gardening, more physical work. More time to learn crafts and useful skills like cooking. This is indeed the experience of parents who have taken this step: when learning is undertaken voluntarily by the child, and when it is done in small groups, then learning progresses quickly. This leaves more idling time, time to run free, unsupervised. It also helps the child to develop the qualities of fearlessness, self-reliance, courage and confidence, which are marks of the child schooled in idleness.

The principle here is to free your mind. There are many alternatives to full-time state education. And the freedom seeker must start with a big question: Do most secondary schools educate, or do they bore kids into submission and prepare them for a powerless life of jobs and money worries? We idlers want to be free of all that. Liberals will argue that state education is good, and certainly there are people from working-class backgrounds who are grateful for their education. But perhaps these are people who would have educated themselves anyway? The bright ones, like Dr. Johnson. And there are likely to be more examples of people who went to state schools who have been reduced to a state of slavery.

Every child should be encouraged to follow his or her own path through life. Indeed, when we look at some of our best thinkers, it is striking how many didn't go to school but were self-taught or taught by tutors: Bertrand Russell, Aldous Huxley (left Eton at sixteen when his eyesight failed), William Blake, William Cobbett and John Stuart Mill all fall into this category. In Tudor times schools tended to spring up around a particular teacher who had moved to the area and might last only a few years. The system was immensely flexible. This is the sort of system I look forward to, one of total flexibility and freedom. We must create our own new schools. We must take education into our own hands, whether that means changing existing schools or creating new ones. And we don't have to wait to be given permission by anyone. We can do what we want.

7.

The Myth of Toys

Toys of silver, gold, coral, cut crystal, rattles of every price and kind; what vain and useless appliances. Away with them all!

Rousseau, *Émile*

hate toys. Toys are toil! In the idle parent's utopia all toys would be banned. No Polly Pockets, no Hungry Hungry Hippos, no Operation, no Lego, no Mega Bloks, no Fuzzy Felt, no Bob the Builder jigsaws, no Mousetrap. (Especially not the new, much worse Mousetrap. What was wrong with the old one?) In other words, no tiny plastic pieces scattered to the four corners of the sitting room. No tiny pieces that you have to clear up at the end of the day because children, in their joy (and rightly), don't care about mess. Little tiny plastic pieces that pierce your feet when you stumble around the house with a hangover, that you trip over on the stairs, that you sit on. Once I waited till the kids were all at school and their mother was also out. With great pleasure, I filled three black bags with old toys and left them by the garbage bins. And the amazing thing was, no one ever noticed. Not one single toy from that pile was ever missed. This indicates that perhaps we are more materialistic than our children. They say they want such-and-such a toy, but their desire is temporary. Perhaps they are more interested in the realization of a wish than the ownership of the object. Parents are more aware of the sweat and the toil that have been expended in order to purchase a particular toy. Toys are money, toys are work, toys are mess, and toys merely console the child for the awful tragedy of having being born into a world that tortures itself with hard work only to relieve the boredom with costly leisure.

How my heart soared when my friend Murphy told how she'd been scanning the aisles for Christmas presents for her daughter. She considered buying a Lego set and then decided against it, because she had looked into the future and seen herself on her hands and knees tidying up hundreds of Lego pieces. Wise, very wise.

There is something dreadful, too, about the way plastic ages. Why is a secondhand plastic toy at a garage sale such a sad sight? Perhaps because in that one bit of scarred and dusty oil-based product is encapsulated the failure of the plastic dream, the abandonment of pleasure and beauty in favor of quantity and cheapness and perhaps a few moments of quiet. In that toy is expressed criminal waste.

So throw them away. Better still, don't buy them in the first place. NO PLASTIC: the cry must go up. The thing is, though, it is so very difficult. Everything is made of plastic. Those toys look so enticing, so cheap, so cheerful when they're on the supermarket shelf. "Hours of fun," they promise, and suggest that this toy is so well thought out, so ingenious, so costly in research and development, so utterly absorbing and delightful that it will practically do the child care for you. But in actual fact, most of these toys demand an enormous amount of input from the parents. Like so many other products of the military-industrial complex, they promise to deliver us from toil, in this case the supposed toil of being with children, but in reality they create more work, both because of the money needed to buy them and the time needed to tidy them up.

And do children actually need toys? In *The Jungle Book* we see Mowgli happily playing with pebbles. The best games are those children play in groups without toys: that's when you hear the laughter. And everyone knows that small children, not yet corrupted by advertising and the whole consumer culture, are happy with a wooden spoon and a saucepan. Children get more fun from a cardboard box than from a pile of toxic toys, beeping their machine-like versions of nursery rhymes (maybe because the child's caregiver is too busy to sing them herself). With the cardboard box, the child's imagination is released. Yesterday my kids made a cardboard box into a space rocket for their cuddly toys. And cardboard boxes can make excellent little playpens: before Arthur could walk we used to put him in a cardboard box and give him a wooden spoon. This left us free to get on with jobs around the kitchen. (By the way, here's a tip: Don't buy any baby machinery. Nothing. We wasted hundreds on absurd devices, like the thing that they sit in and use to walk around the room. No: they learn how to walk on their own.)

Left alone, children will find and make their own toys, and in the process will develop their creativity rather than relying on entertainment from costly gadgets made by greedy toy manufacturers. You—the parents—you can make your own toys too. Yes, you can. This is a noble calling for the dad of the family. Buy a saw and a chisel (we'll return to the joys of wood later). Cut out airplane shapes from that fantastic modeling material, cardboard. Get some gaffer tape. (Arthur has just made his own catapult out of cardboard, gaffer tape and an elastic band. He has called it the Slinger 3000.) Make puppets out of socks and buttons. Monster masks from paper bags. It's amazing what you can do with little or no skill in this department. Get them used to making things from an early age. Our non-plastic homemade toys, unlike bought plastic ones, can be mended, improved, painted, taken apart and remade. And burned, if necessary.

Rousseau was also against toys, though the toys in his day were not plastic:

> Let us have no corals or rattles; a small branch of a tree with its leaves and fruit, a stick of licorice which he may suck and chew, will amuse him as well as these splendid trifles, and they will have this advantage at least, he will not be brought up to luxury from his birth.

The message is clear: don't waste time and money on toys when you can simply pluck a branch from a tree and give it to the child. He will use his imagination to play with it, to slay monsters with it, eat it or make it into a pig. Clearly this route is also the ecologically friendly option: no planet-wasting plastic, just a piece of nature, free, easy and very green. Yes, idle parenting will save the planet.

Toys mean play commodified. They are part of the consumer society, and the sensible person rejects the consumer society because, very simply, it entails too much effort. The idle parent can't be bothered. Not buying and not working—in other words, making and living—is in actual fact easier and cheaper. Yes, make your own. A hobby horse is a bit of cloth tied to the top of a stick, and really can provide hours of fun.

All of this is not to reject play. A child's life is, or should be, about play, and in fact they can teach the adults how to play. It is wonderful to watch them play. The Elizabethan philosopher John Dee writes the following charming entry in his diary: "Arthur Dee and May Herbert, they being but three yere old the eldest, did make as it were a shew of childish marriage, of calling each other husband and wife."

Games and play do not require toys. Money does not equal fun, as A. S. Neill remarks in an anecdote about his daughter Zoë:

Once Zoë received a gift from an old pupil of a wonderful walking and talking doll. It was obviously an expensive toy. About the same time, a new pupil gave Zoë a small cheap rabbit. She played with the big expensive doll for about half an hour, but she played with the cheap little rabbit for weeks.

Neill, too, thinks we spend far too much money on toys. We're hoodwinked by the toy companies, who encourage us to buy things as an expression of love.

Every nursery is filled with toys that are broken and neglected. Every middle-class child gets far too many toys. In fact, most toys that cost more than a few pennies are wasted. All parents have a tendency to overbuy toys. Baby eagerly holds out his hands toward some gadget—a tractor, a giraffe that nods—and parents buy it on the spot. Thus most nurseries are full of toys in which the child never shows any real interest.

Television and computers are partly to blame. When Arthur used to watch TV, he would come into the kitchen having been seduced by an advertisement for some gadget and ask if he could have it. "It's only nineteen ninety-nine!" he argued. There are some campaigners, I understand, who argue that kids' television should be ad-free, because children are so susceptible to the hidden persuaders. Good luck to them. While they are fighting that battle, we just unplug.

Shopping trips into town are hellish. The harried parent wastes vitality by saying "no" constantly and is also made to feel mean and stingy. The answer is to limit your kids' exposure to advertising and also to avoid, if at all possible, trips to town. I find that sweets are better than toys as gifts. They are just as delighted with sweets as with toys—if not more so—and the sweets have the inestimable advantage of being self-destroying. They leave no trace, particularly if you are lucky enough to have access to a shop that sells them loose, so the kids can fill a little paper bag with their own selection.

Be mean. Locke, too, was concerned that a surfeit of stuff would only serve to spoil children and make them want more:

> I have known a young child so distracted with the number and variety of his play-games, that he tired his maid every day to look them over; and was so accustomed to abundance that he never thought he had enough, but was always asking, What more? What more? What new thing shall I have?

So we see the seeds of the consumer society being sown back in 1693. Locke recommends that "they should have none bought for them . . . they should make them themselves." So it seems that Locke was as anticonsumerist as any modern-day environmentalist:

> A smooth pebble, a piece of paper, the mother's bunch of keys, or anything they cannot hurt themselves with, serves as much to divert little children as those more chargeable and curious toys from the shops, which are presently put out of order and broken.

What a sensible man. What on earth is the point of spending money on expensive toys that you will worry about and which will get broken anyway? And why do relatives insist on giving expensive presents? "This is a very special thing, Arthur. You will look after it, won't you?" Arthur nods obligingly, but you might as well have been singing the National Anthem for all the moral instruction he will have received. He'll be just as careless with it as with anything else—and that's good. Surely that shows a healthy disrespect for manufactured objects and the whole panoply of consumer baubles?

While Locke and Rousseau were lucky in that they didn't have to deal with the horrors of plastic, the basic issues remain unchanged. So I repeat: throw it away. Don't buy it. Keep it simple. Make your own. Accustom them not to abundance. Particularly when they are small and have not yet been seduced by the commercial world. You can save a lot of money when they're young. My friend Dan said he felt mean because he had spent "only" $150 on his two-year-old's Christmas presents. One hundred fifty dollars? That would keep me in real ale for nearly a month. Was he crazy? Ten bucks would have sufficed. As if the kid would know the difference. Keep your cash while they are small. It will be more difficult later on. Take pleasure in exercising your revolutionary duty. Stop buying, and a new world of pleasure and creativity awaits you.

One toy that I do approve of is the wooden train set. To build tracks using this stuff can actually be quite enjoyable for adults as well as kids. The train set, being wooden, does not offend the parents' aesthetic sense as violently as plastic rubbish. And you can buy more trains and buy more track. Friends and relatives can add to it. We started with a small set for Arthur, and now Henry plays with a wonderfully elaborate system. (One tip: Avoid the battery-powered engines. They run out. All the time. And you have to find or buy new batteries. And fit them, which requires a tiny screwdriver, which is not always easy to find. I hate batteries.) The wooden nature of the train set means that somehow tidying it up is not such an irksome chore as tidying up plastic toys.

And it's true that there are some beautiful things out there, made with love and skill. So save your money by avoiding the mass-produced rubbish and buying instead the occasional good-quality item.

Keep it simple. Here is a list of medieval toys that archaeologists have found, according to childhood historian Colin Heywood. We might do well to stick to them: "Rattles, wooden tops, spun by a whip or the fingers, dolls, miniature cooking utensils and dinner sets in ceramic or base metals, model boats, lead soldiers, little clay animals."

The fewer the toys, the better. Then your child will be unspoiled and rich in imagination.

8.

Ban TV, Embrace Freedom

The optical projection dominates the world, but it is only one way of seeing, and one that separates us from the world.

David Hockney, *Secret Knowledge*, 2001

s it possible to ban TV without banning TV? In this chapter, I want to explore how to remove the pernicious influence of evil television while not banning all screen-based entertainment. After all, who could deny the genius of *The Simpsons*? And who wants to ban things? That's what Puritans and governments do. And the idle parent has to confess that the television can be quite handy if you want some peace and quiet to drink a cup of tea, have a doze or putter in the garden.

But really, the television is bad. It is useless. It is disabling. Firstly, there is the absurd expense. One hears that people are spending over $4,000 on a giant plasma screen. Add to that the annual subscription charge for cable service, which could be around as much as $1,000 a year—well, taking the average income as $4,000 a month, you're talking about more than a month's worth of work. A month! Which you could take off and spend doing nothing! No wonder television advertises debt reconciliation companies nonstop. The television itself has created a debt-heavy nation and the television now tries to solve the problem it has created. Or as Homer Simpson says: "The answer to life's problems aren't at the bottom of a bottle. They're on TV!" Television also encourages the spending of money, the natural result of the constant advertising that beams from the screen. It actively and ingeniously works to create a series of wants. It is said by free market libertarians that big supermarkets do not force people into their shops at gunpoint. No. But they do something far more pernicious, which is to brainwash millions of people by firing advertisements at them in the break in the middle of a soap opera. All those millions are hit with the most sophisticated marketing techniques known to mankind. The marketing departments of the supermarkets employ the country's finest brains to manipulate us. So it's no wonder that we think the supermarkets are wonderful. The butcher, the baker and the candlestick maker don't really stand a chance, with no budget for television spending.

So banning TV will make you richer overnight and it will remove a host of temptations. You will no longer be advertised at and neither will your children. The financial savings are incalculable. Put the money you've saved toward reducing time spent at work: you will have more time for loafing, lollygagging and staring at the ceiling. The advertisers get parents into an "emotional vice" as Victoria puts it. You want your kids to fit in with the other kids and therefore you buy them rubbish. (My parents were lucky because when I was a teenager, thrift-shop clothes were fashionable.) But the rubbish costs money, and to get the money you have to work. And then, because you are all tired from overwork, you collapse in front of the television every night, exhausted and susceptible to suggestion. You watch it for three hours every day and then complain that there aren't enough hours in the day. There would be more hours in the day if you quit telly. Plus it makes you grumpy.

I don't make an exception for educational programs. Many middle-class parents think that so-called educational television is superior to *South Park*. That is completely wrong. Television is a medium, human beings are artists, and some of these artists have created art in TV form. *South Park*, *The Simpsons*, and *The Sopranos* may be some examples. *Barney*, though, is not art. It is patronizing. Better to watch good-quality telly in bad taste than bad-quality telly in good taste.

Worse still, so many children's programs promote the capitalist work ethic. Think of the busy world of Richard Scarry, where everyone is encouraged to be gainfully employed and there are no lazy people. Bob the Builder is the foremost example of the plot to brainwash children in this way. "Can we fix it? Yes we can," goes the glib catchphrase (strange, actually, because building is supposed to be about making things, not just fixing broken ones). In Arthur's early years, we used to watch a lot of television. I remember sitting there at 5:30 a.m., in my underpants, watching hours of rubbish and thinking, "What the hell am I doing?" I remember one particularly chilling episode of *Bob the Builder* in which Bob gave his machines the day off—but they came to work anyway! Just for fun! So servile were they that they had no idea what to do with themselves when released, and willingly put their time back into the control of their master. What kind of message is that sending out to kids?

Clearly watching television is passive: instead of playing their own games, the children are meekly submitting to somebody else's creation. As David Hockney points out in his brilliant study of the use of lenses in Renaissance art, *Secret Knowledge*, telly, compared with a still painting, is a tyrant: "Film and video bring their time to us; we bring our time to painting." You cannot contemplate the television. It imposes on us.

In his book *The Disappearance of Childhood*, the social critic Neil Postman makes the point that watching television is not a skill. You do not become better at it if you do it more often. He also points out that it is a negative medium: for example, soap operas show the adult world to be full of strife, pain, misery and rage (Plato had the same objection to the poetry of his time). You could argue that television is a mechanized storytelling device, a sort of magic lantern, and what's wrong with that, but the stories that are broadcast are either quite horrifying or so bland as to be practically nonexistent. Then, after you have watched the bad news of the soap opera and television news, as Marshall McLuhan puts it, the commercials are the good news. Life bad? Well, buy this and it will get better!

Television also encourages blind belief in technological progress. It constantly expresses the dominant ideology of the West, which is: Technology Will Save Us (a false notion first put about by deluded writers such as H. G. Wells). Says Postman: "In TV-commercial parables the root cause of evil is Technological Innocence, a failure to know the particulars of the beneficent accomplishments of industrial progress." Technology has become a god, and TV and the Internet are the modern means of spreading the gospel, as was the printed word for the Puritans. If you don't believe, then turn it off. The medium is the message, and the message is: Put up with your boring job and then splurge your wages on useless rubbish. The more both children and adults are kept away from this propaganda, the better.

But let's not get too fanatical: at home we have kept the telly for watching DVDs and videos. We love *The Simpsons*, of course, but also great old movies like *Great Expectations* and my favorite of all time, *Mutiny on the Bounty* with Marlon Brando as Fletcher Christian. Videos are a thrifty buy: they cost next to nothing in charity shops. As I have argued elsewhere, it is possible to live luxuriously on small amounts of money—you just have to go backward ten years. Go back five hundred years and you can literally live like a king.

A further problem is that adults have invaded the playground. Just as kids' television is created by committees of highly paid adult executives who make money, more or less directly, from the brands who advertise on their shows, kids' games are being taken over by adults. This process is particularly advanced in the United States. Children's games are disappearing, Postman reports, replaced by "highly organized, expensive and adult-operated sports clubs like Little League baseball and Pee Wee football." Americans are "insisting that even at age six, children play their games without spontaneity, under careful supervision, and at an intense competitive level. . . . Children's play has become an adult preoccupation, it has become professionalized, it is no longer a world separate from the adults."

Give childhood back to the children. Resist the American way. Keep rebelling! Make family life into a revolutionary act. This is the message of Postman's excellent book:

> Specifically, resistance entails conceiving of parenting as an act of rebellion against American culture. . . . Most rebellious of all is the attempt to control the media's access to one's children. There are, in fact, two ways to do this. The first is to limit the amount of exposure children have to media. The second is to monitor carefully what they are exposed to, and to provide them with a continuously running critique of the themes and values of the media's content.

And the easy way to do this is to throw the telly out of the window. We have now finally unplugged, and it is a great liberation. The children rarely ask for it back, and they read and play instead. And of course we can still watch movies and collected TV shows on DVD and video. This means we can watch good stuff at times of our choosing with little or no ads.

Then, of course, there is the Internet. It seems that you can watch all sorts of stuff via the Web. Arthur, for example, found some great old Beatles clips on YouTube, and we greatly enjoyed watching them together. With broadband there really is no excuse for television at all. TV is dead.

Last month the kids had neither telly nor computer, as both were broken. After a couple of days, they got used to this, and after school, instead of dashing to a screen, they were to be found drawing at the kitchen table or making things or playing self-invented games. There is no doubt that minimizing screen time maximized their inner resources. This is good for the present because they are enjoying themselves properly. But it's also good for the kids' future: they will be able to snap their fingers at employers and do their own thing. Television breeds incapable people.

So save money, improve your life, improve your kids' life. No more telly and limit screen time. But again, let's not be too fanatical. *Tom and Jerry* on video or *The Simpsons* on DVD: we'll make an exception for those.

9.

Let Us Sleep

I used to think booze and sex would bring me joy. Now it's a nap.

P. J. O'ROURKE

The most trying aspect of being a parent is the disruption to your sleep. As someone who had been accustomed to his nine or ten hours a night in pre-kid days, I found the sleep loss hard to deal with. It is undeniable that in a culture where to be a hardworking family is an aspiration, sleep in general is devalued. Successful high-achievers boast about how little sleep they need. We would rather drink giant cups of coffee or take pep pills, herbal or otherwise, to boost ourselves through the day than accept nature's call and simply take a short nap. In any culture or situation, though, where we are in control of our own time, we tend to take naps and sleep a lot. Think of those long, luxurious siestas that you manage to take on holiday. Ah, the nap! We lust after naps. Naps are a paradise.

And rightly so, because lack of sleep is a terrible thing. I remember when our eldest child was small waking in the night to find him kicking my back. We'd attempted to "get him into a routine" as current child-care orthodoxy suggests, and failed. He was in bed with us again. I wish instead we'd embraced co-sleeping right from the start. Babies should be held as much as possible when they are small, by Mom, Dad or anyone who is around. Parents can have sex in the bathroom. Routines, separate rooms and strict nanny regimes are the enemy of the idle parent. I know, because we have tried them. Our copy of a certain guide to getting your baby into a routine is the most battered and dog-eared book I've ever seen, so frequently was it consulted by the nervous mother. Strict routines are intended to give the parents some peace and to get the baby to sleep well, but this was not our experience. The routines seemed to set the baby up as an enemy, to be controlled, abandoned, separated, confined, ignored. And they were extremely hard work: so complex that V talked of nothing else for a year. It was exasperating. There is only one book on babies that you should read, if you read any at all, and that is *The Continuum Concept* (we'll come back to that later).

Nights of being kicked in the kidneys and screaming and saying "your turn" to the other parent create serious sleep loss, particularly if you make the other mistake that I did, which was to work in an office all day, a long way from home. I found it very difficult to catch up. No chance for a nap. It would make me grumpy. Very grumpy. Enraged would be a more accurate description of my mood. Livid. Then in the evening we would drink, in an attempt to inject a little bit of pleasure into our lives. Then at night I would be woken by Arthur's surprisingly heavy hand flopping on to my face. For eight years, we've had sleeping problems. At one point everyone seemed to wake up in the morning in a different bed from the one they'd gone to sleep in. I have woken up in children's beds, in the spare room, on the sofa. During the night, various children have taken my place. One friend said that his family of four ended up in a sort of square formation, one along each edge of the double bed.

We still have the occasional broken night. But it's so much better now. The eldest two have been trained—the idle parent way, by their parents simply staying in bed—to get dressed and make their own breakfast without disturbing us. The smallest one still sometimes ends up in our bed. But it's fun! So, although I'm not fond of handing out top tips, because this book really is about a single general principle which you can apply to your life in your own way, I thought it might be useful to pass on a few ideas garnered from our long, hard years of experience of kids and sleep.

(a) Going to Bed Early

Clearly, for the idle parent, going to bed early seems a little, well, square. When the small ones have finally gone to sleep, following an elaborate ritual consisting of bath, massage, story time, lullabies, platelets of sliced fruit and beakers of water, it's surely time for Mom and Dad to indulge in a little pleasure? This is the time when I generally drink as much beer as I can. And with each subsequent beer, the desire to go to bed recedes. Why would I want to go to bed now, when I've finally started enjoying myself? But we've found over the years that unless we were in bed by half past ten, particularly if there was a child under two in the house, we'd find the daytime almost intolerable. And we'd get angry with each other. It's temporary, and I think there's some comfort in that knowledge. The whole thing gets easier when the youngest is past two and a half or so. The way, though, to make going to bed early enjoyable is to have a good book on the go. As far as pure pleasure in reading goes, I don't think Keats can be beaten, and that goes for his letters or poetry. He's got a sort of cheerful melancholy which is immensely comforting. And he's also a great lover of sleep, of course. I suppose the other good reason for an early night is sex, however rarely that seems to be in the cards. Going to bed early can become a pleasure rather than a penance, and whether that pleasure is found in reading, sex, cocoa, writing poetry or reading the seed catalogue is of no account. But it should be the ongoing goal of the idle parent to inject pleasure into the day, constantly. It is one of the tragedies of serious Western attitudes to raising children that fun and enjoyment seem to vanish from the agenda in favor of moneymaking and conversation about the kids. Do not become a slave to your children! You will become resentful and they will hate you for it.

(b) The Sleep-in

Yes, I know that this is easier said than done. But this last summer holiday, quite remarkably, we found ourselves lying in bed till ten or eleven on several occasions, and this with children aged three, six and eight in the house. Sometimes, agreed, they would come and wake us by doing horrible things, jumping on our legs, "rampaging" as we called it, and hitting each other. But after we'd chucked them out a few times, they began to look after themselves. They are all quite capable of pouring milk on cereal, and Arthur, as I boasted earlier, can make tea and porridge. Children actually have a built-in self-protective sense that we destroy by overcosseting. Children become independent not so much by careful training but in part simply as a result of parental laziness. Last Sunday morning Victoria and I lay in bed till half past ten with hangovers. What a result! And the more often you do this, the better, because the children's resourcefulness will improve, resulting in less nagging, less of that awful "Mom-eeeeeeh" noise they make. They can play and they will play. So lying in bed for as long as possible is not the act of an irresponsible parent. It is precisely the opposite: it is good to look after yourself—the idle parent, I say again, must constantly guard against resentment—and it is good to teach the children to fend for themselves. Our offspring will be strong, bold, fearless, much in demand wherever they go! Capable, cheerful, happy. It is also the task of the idle parent to ensure as far as possible that all members of the family are enjoying themselves here and now, in the present moment. There is far too much emphasis on that imprisoning capitalist abstraction "the future." Yes, we have one eye on future adulthood, but the best way to ensure that the adulthood is happy is to provide a happy childhood. Not a competitive one, filled with prizes and awards or the wasteful ephemera of capitalist overproduction. No. A happy one, with plenty of everything: love, music, games, laughter galore. There is no point in sacrificing pleasurable todays for the promise of more prosperous tomorrows. So stay in that bed as much as you can.

(c) Take a Nap

All over the world, the sane take a nap after lunch. I don't need to convince you, idle reader, of the many pleasures and many benefits to health and well-being of an hour's nap each day. It is so important—particularly when the kids are small—that I would go so far as to say this: if you have a job which makes it impossible to have a nap—a full-time job far from home, for example—then quit that job. I regret spending too much time in the office when Arthur was small, and Victoria and I also frequently reflect on how much better our life would have been if we had bought a small flat near the office rather than a house one hour away. Victoria was working in the same area of London as I was, so we would leave Arthur with a babysitter, trek across town, and then come back again. If we had lived near our places of work, we could have ensured a greater crossover between work and home. We could have popped back for lunch and a nap and even taken Arthur into work sometimes. Later I changed my work situation and started working from home, and that was a great improvement.

So, quit that job. Your health and happiness and that of your family are more important than the profits of the corporation that you slave for. You don't need much money. "Eat nettles!" as the

Austrian artist and architect Friedensreich Hundertwasser suggested. There are a host of books out there that can show you how to live well and plentifully on small amounts of money, and your own imagination is a wonderful resource.

Taking a nap with your little kids is also a great pleasure: it's like sleeping with a small hot-water-bottle teddy-bear creature. And they do look cute when asleep. Father can put his feet up by the fire and nod off while reading "Ode on Melancholy," retreat into dreamland and wake refreshed. All right—you do not work at home. And you can't quit your job. Then take a pillow to the office. Sleep in the back of a church in your lunch hour, stretched out along a pew in the delicious cool. Nap on a park bench or under a tree. Indulge in daytime sexual reveries. I heard recently of a New York company that is attempting to combat our sleep shortage with a power-nap service. After lunch you enter the nap emporium, where you are shown to a comfy reclining chair in a dark room. Ambient sounds help you drift off to sleep and then wake you after the allotted twenty minutes. The problem here, of course, is that the nap costs money. So typical of New York to commodify something that is actually free: sleep! This kind of nap center built on a troubling premise: purportedly the nap will return you to the office refreshed, in order that you can toil more effectively for your paymasters. It is a power nap, taken not for its own pleasure but in order to serve the capitalist machine and make you more productive. Well, that is not the motivation for the idle parent's naps. We take our naps because we enjoy our lives. And it is for that reason that partners should make it a rule to ensure that the other one enjoys as many naps as possible. We should not begrudge our wife or husband a siesta. It is all too easy to slip into that slavish, resentful morality whereby we imagine that the other person somehow has it easier. I can't stand that dreadful evening standoff where each partner tries to convince the other that his or her own life is harder. We should be overjoyed when our partner naps; the partner is not slacking off, but merely being sensible. We need sleep!

Sleep-deprived people lack reason. They are dark shadows of gloom. They become tetchy and irritable. Everyone seems an idiot, and the world is hostile. One friend says he gets into a sort of murderous rage, and he doesn't realize that his fury is directly caused by his lack of sleep until he finally gets some rest. Then he wakes up and feels like a different person. Sleep is a care-charmer. So follow the Spanish, the Mexicans, the Africans. Wherever people have a greater degree of control over their everyday lives, they nap. It was common to see workers in China napping by the roadside till recently. Sleep will make you strong and beautiful. If there are any idle-friendly employers out there (which I doubt), then introduce nap rooms into your office. We are always banging on about how rich we are in the West, yet we cannot organize our time efficiently enough to allow ourselves a nap in the day. What fools. Let us sleep. As soon as the first baby is born, prioritize the nap. Make that first couple of years together a pleasant sleep-filled haze.

(d) Take a Sleep Holiday

Could you possibly ask that great unpaid team of volunteers—friends, relatives and neighbors—to look after the kids for a few hours so that you can nap? I don't know why we are so fearful about admitting that we need to rest. We organize child care so we can work or go out in the evening. But sleeping somehow seems less essential. Victoria and I hired a nanny so we could nap. Au pairs, babysitters or nannies are the commodified version of the extended family. In more sane societies, child care is shared among large numbers of people, reducing the burden on individual parents and creating wide margins for error, margins in which sleep can be inserted. Marvel at the guilt-free, hammock-based nap of the Mexican parent, safe in the knowledge that their children are surrounded by friends and family. The nuclear family is exhausting. The lonely parent is tired. Therefore gather people around you. You need callers all day long. They will help; they will wash up. Don't feel you have to entertain. Some of my readers have criticized me for hiring an au pair, arguing that I should take my own advice and spend less and work less. But for us, nannies and au pairs were a way of extending the family. They were not a necessity since both of us were at home most of the time. Sometimes we did it on our own. Out of eight years, we had full- or half-time help for four. And did it alone for the other four. The nanny and au pair allowed us time for naps and sleep and pleasure. And they provided company too. We afforded them by extending our mortgage! That's how reckless we were. But it was worth it, just not to feel completely exhausted all the time. And for the children, it was far better to have that continuity of care (nanny Claire was here for three years) than to be dumped in nurseries from a young age (and indeed, we found we were spending less on a full-time nanny than some friends were spending on nurseries). And there really is no comparison, as far as fun for the kids goes, between a nanny and nursery.

Best of all, though, is to do it with friends and family, to arrange swaps and organize your own little day-care group. You could organize a rotation and do it at different local parents' houses. Help each other with the cleaning too. Why should all household work be done alone? That is the worst part of it. Organize a laundry day. Put the children on the floor and do the laundry together.

If you want more sleep, then you must also abandon that other fiendish invention of capitalist parenting orthodoxy: Family Days Out, which make it impossible to take a nap.

You cannot nip off for an hour while standing in line at a theme park. In fact, shouldn't theme parks introduce free nap rooms for parents? Surely that would swell numbers.

One dad friend of mine has a neat trick. He takes his three boys to the cinema after lunch to give his wife a break. Having deposited the boys in front of the screen, he then returns to the car, puts the seat down and goes to sleep for an hour or two. This is genius: he saves the money for his own ticket, he doesn't have to sit through an American animation, he has given his wife a break, and he has a good sleep as part of the bargain. Now, that's idle parenting.

We should not wait for the government or our employer or a partner to grant us sleep. We must simply exercise our sleep rights without asking. Do not petition, just take. Sleep is free, sleep is a gift, sleep is good. It is not directly useful to the economy, and that is why the idle parent recognizes that a lot of it is essential to the individual. From lack of sleep results many evils: door-slammings, shoutings, swearings, miscarriages of justice and unhappiness.

We need to accustom ourselves to calling the neighbors and saying without fear or shame: "Can you keep an eye on the kids for an hour or two? I need a nap." We need to give each other breaks, frequent little holidays from the nuclear family.

(e) Put a Mattress on the Floor by the Bed

This was a very helpful strategy that I hit on during our toddler years. Before I discovered it, I would begin each night sleeping in the marital bed. But all too often, someone would wake me up by slapping me in the face or kicking me in the back. And, after lying there for half an hour trying to get back to sleep, I would stomp off to the spare room in a rage. So I made up a little bed and laid it alongside the main bed. Now if a child came in to wake me, I simply rolled off the big bed and into my snug little burrow. I suggested this trick to my friend Marcel and he says it works very well. He rolls over into his nest with great pleasure: "It's not much," he says, "but it's mine."

(f) Separate Rooms

By the time we'd had our third child, there was no room for senti-ment. I moved straight out, and for ten months or so I slept in the spare room. This way at least one of us was not sleep-deprived. And there are great pleasures to be had in sleeping alone. You can read as late as you like; you wake up when you wake up. Some mornings I was really lucky, and Victoria would bring me a cup of tea at 7:30 a.m.—bliss! For her part, she was able to nap in the afternoon, and catch up on sleep that way. Because I was not tired, I was able to help with child care and cleaning during the day. Our idea was that Victoria should spend as much time in bed as she could with the baby during his first few months and as little time as possible worrying about housework.

(g) All in the Same Room

Another strategy I have heard about is for every adult and child to sleep in the same room, the idea being that when a child wakes up, she will feel warm and secure in the company of the others and will simply go back to sleep. Again, this is something that can be experimented with. Move mattresses in and out of the main bedroom, try different approaches. Probably the very worst of all is to put the young baby in its crib alone in a nursery next door. As for sleeping with baby, this may be a matter of practice: in *The Continuum Concept*, Jean Liedloff says that parents don't give it a proper go. This may be true, but anecdotal evidence suggests that parents find it hard to sleep with a toddler writhing around in the bed.

But however you do it, the message is clear: More sleep required.

10.

The Power of Music
and Dancing

Maxima debetur puero reverentia.
(Children are entitled to the greatest respect.)
JUVENAL, *Satires* (first–second century A.D.)

One thing that strikes me when reading John Locke's *Some Thoughts Concerning Education*, or when studying accounts of everyday life in medieval Europe, or indeed when reading anthropological reports about the customs of contemporary tribes, or even reading about English life as little as one hundred years ago, is the amount of dancing and singing that goes on. Right into the eighteenth century it was customary for children to have singing and dancing lessons at home. Adults, too, had dancing masters—often caricatured in Hogarth prints as skinny, effete Italians. Coleridge writes of after-dinner dancing as a routine occurrence in his account of life in Nether Stowey,

Somerset, around 1798. People danced nearly every night. Locke recommended dancing lessons from a young age, partly as a means of instilling confidence:

> And since nothing appears to me to give children so much becoming confidence and behavior, and so to raise them to the conversation of those above their age, as dancing, I think they should be taught to dance as soon as they are capable of learning. For though this consist only in outward gracefulness of motion, yet, I know not how, it gives children manly thoughts and carriage more than anything.

It is important to remember that Locke's ideal child is home-taught. Therefore his advice is not aimed at schools, on to whom we customarily shift responsibility for the education of our children today, but at parents. And so it is today: if we want our children to dance, we must arrange it ourselves—do not wait for the government to do it.

It is terrible to be someone like me in matters of dancing. I watch others dance with envy and it is generally only after I've ingested large amounts of alcohol that I lose my inhibitions enough to venture on to the dance floor. Once there I rehearse a couple of dimly remembered moves picked up in my raving days, when we used to dance all night in warehouses. But this lack of confidence is not a result of innate uselessness, as most of us think. It is a direct consequence of never having been taught how to dance. Just as I would be nervous to drive a car without having had lessons, so I am nervous to tread on the dance floor untutored. But if we'd all been taught dancing and practiced it all our lives, then we would have sufficient confidence. We'd have a repertoire of moves. Dancing is not actually spontaneous: it needs to be learned and practiced. Those break dancers, those carnival paraders, those rock'n'rollers, those waltzers and tangoers: they've been practicing. We are still a Puritan culture and the Puritans (most of them) frowned on dancing as an indulgent pleasure wholly irrelevant to salvation. For other religious cultures, of course, dancing is absolutely central to the whole experience. It's fascinating to note that the ecstatic, pleasure-loving "whirling dervishes" branch of Sufism is making a comeback. This Islamic mystical offshoot took the form of various sects, mostly founded in the twelfth and thirteenth centuries in Turkey. One such group, the Mevlana, was founded by the radical Muslim preacher and poet Jalaludinn Rumi. His doctrine preached universal tolerance, and the whirling was about losing the ego. I recommend his collected poetry. It's a good one for the idle parent to have by the bed. He writes things like:

Get drunk on Love, for Love is all that exists. Unless you make Love your business, you will not be admitted to the beloved.

I suppose he was the Lennon of his day. He also writes in favor of living in the now: "The Sufi is the child of the present moment, my friend. The word 'tomorrow' is excluded from the doctrine of those who travel the path." And dancing is a way of connecting with the present moment.

Such ecstatic dancing was not confined to Sufi dervishes. The great Barbara Ehrenreich, in *Dancing in the Streets*, quotes the following description of the goings-on in a twelfth-century Welsh church:

> You can see young men and maidens, some in the church itself, some in the churchyard and others in the dance which wends its way round the graves. They sing traditional songs, all of a sudden they collapse on the ground, and then those who, until now, have followed their leader peacefully as if in a trance, leap up in the air as if seized by frenzy.

Ehrenreich characterizes the medieval period as one long party. Every week or two, she says, there was some kind of festival that involved music and dancing. This is a view shared by the historian Ronald Hutton, who in his work describes the culture of merriment and partying in late medieval England. But then: the clampdown. From the sixteenth through to the nineteenth century, the ecclesiastical tendency to regard dancing and joy and merriment as somewhat suspect, possibly devilish, gains ground, and pleasure begins to be outlawed officially rather than merely disapproved of as before.

There were signs of hope: later, as Aldous Huxley insisted in a recorded interview: "The Quakers *quaked* and the Shakers *shook*," in an attempt to recapture the spiritual joy of physical abandonment. But the general trend was away from dancing and fun: "In the long-term history from the seventeenth to the twentieth century . . . there were literally thousands of acts of legislation introduced which attempted to eliminate carnival and popular festivity from European life." So write historians Peter Stallybrass and Allon White of the effects of the Reformation. Protestantism and the emerging hard-work capitalist culture had no time for festivity. In the new world, where time was money, dancing was to squander, to waste money. Dancing was useless. The Puritans had a new world to build, and time was short. Contemplation, dancing, merriment: these were all simply a waste of time.

In the twentieth century, and into the twenty-first, dancing for many of us is something we watch other people doing on television. We can sometimes be persuaded to pull some moves at weddings or the disco, but the results are usually embarrassing. There is hope in the hip-hop scene and break dancing: kids are teaching themselves the most fantastic routines. But this is still a minority interest, whereas we all used to dance. Now dancing has vanished into the realms of the spectacle. To be sure, pockets of sanity still exist: in the Scottish Islands they still know how to dance, and on many islands there is a weekly ceilidh. Fifteen years ago, on the Greek island of Ithaca, my friends and I stumbled across a village dance, with about two hundred islanders, of all ages, dancing in a huge circle. Lately the rave movement saw an outbreak of ecstatic dancing, but this outbreak of merriment was soon controlled by the double-edged sword of authority; legislate against it, then commodify it. The Criminal Justice and Public Order Act of 1994 made it illegal for groups to gather together for the purposes of dancing, without a license. But at the same time, the commercial world began to exploit the popularity of rave by installing DJs in a nightclub called The Ministry of Sound. Tourists were imported to pump some money into the capital, and the very movement that the authorities had cracked down on became an important source of revenue. Together with a British art boom, it helped to attract big finance into London.

But children dancing for their own pleasure? Children dancing and no one making a profit? People organizing their own dances outside of the commercial system? What's the point? Where is the money to be made? Every school should have dancing lessons every week, twice a week.

It's a similar story with music. Only the hardworking and talented tend to continue with music beyond primary age. And then, unless they get really good, they might be put off for life. Victoria, for example, reached Grade 6 on the piano, but she never goes near one (even though we have a piano in the kitchen) because she still has no confidence. Grade 6 seems not really very good to her (it seems like genius to me). Schools tend to turn out adults with many skills and lots of fear. There is a wrongheaded notion that something's not worth doing unless you're the very best at it, which leads to most of us doing nothing at all.

And self-consciousness gets you quickly. I've noticed that Arthur already seems shy about singing and dancing, whereas younger kids will spontaneously hurl themselves about when the music starts, waving their arms and moving from side to side. I think every house should have music playing all day, and piles of instruments everywhere.

So music and dancing tend to disappear from young lives. It's only when they become teenagers that they pick up their guitars, dye their hair, listen to Nirvana and start playing in bands. And it has to be said, there are a hell of a lot of young people playing in bands these days. That really is an encouraging sign of life.

Before the total commodification of music, whereby music was bought and sold on vinyl or cassette or digital format, we sang for ourselves. Yes, of course there were top composers and performers who were commissioned by grand families and courts to play and write. But in the streets, we all sang. If you walked down the street in fourteenth-century Florence, for example, many centuries before the invention of the wireless, you would see every artisan singing outside his own workshop, as the following story about Dante testifies:

> One day in Florence, [after eating, Dante] came upon "a smith who was beating iron on the anvil and singing Dante the way one sings a popular poem, and mixing his verses up, shortening some and lengthening others, so that it seemed to Dante that he was receiving a great injury from the fellow." Without a word Dante went into the man's workshop and threw his tongs, his hammer, his balances, and all his other implements into the street. . . . "You are singing from my work, but not the way I wrote it; I have no other art [skill, trade], and you are ruining it for me." The irate smith, at a loss for words, gathered up his things and went back to his work; and after that, when he wanted to sing, he sang of Tristan and Lancelot, and left Dante alone.

So, how to bring music and dancing back into our lives and the lives of our children? As far as music goes, I have started to teach the ukulele at our local primary school. The uke is an ideal starter instrument for children because it is small and easy to play. Most children can learn "Twinkle, Twinkle, Little Star" and the chord of C in about half an hour. So you get good results quickly, unlike, say, with the violin. Having to teach the children also motivates me to practice and to think about the instrument. The other great things about the uke are that any number of kids can play it at the same time and, unlike the dreaded recorder, it leaves the mouth free for singing. It is also cheap: good ones can be bought for $35.

The ukulele is by nature cheerful. It was born when Portuguese immigrants to Hawaii in the late nineteenth century jumped off the boat playing small Portuguese guitars. The Hawaiians adapted these instruments and soon the whole island was playing them, including the Hawaiian royal family. Therefore they embody a sort of joyful Hawaiian spirit.

The ukulele encourages a rhythmic sort of playing style, which means you can get people dancing without the need for drums. At a recent wedding I attended, the PA briefly malfunctioned and the music stopped. To fill the gap I strummed a few chords on the uke, and everyone continued dancing.

Music can also happen spontaneously. Yesterday I was conducting an all-day leave-them-alone educational experiment, which consisted of my lying on the sofa, dozing and reading, while the children busied themselves around me. Henry played with a tractor and trailer; Delilah talked to herself in a delightful sing-song voice. Arthur, who is generally the telly- and computer-addicted one, played with the pots and pans all day. First he put a colander on his head and sat on a pile of pots, saying: "I am the pots-and-pans king." Later he arranged the pots in another heap and banged them in turn with a wooden spoon. "I've made a musical instrument." However, Arthur seems terribly inhibited when it comes to dancing. I don't know why. Maybe he has already lost the wild and uninhibited nature of small children.

You could go even further and remove them from any kind of formal music and give them more exposure to the music of nature. This is the line taken by Masanobu Fukuoka, that great Japanese natural farmer I mentioned earlier.

In raising children, many parents make the same mistake as I made in the orchard at first. For example, teaching music to children is as unnecessary as pruning orchard trees. A child's ear catches the music. The murmuring of a stream, the sound of frogs croaking by the riverbank, the rustling of leaves in the forest, all these natural sounds are music—true music. However, when a variety of disturbing noises enters and confuses the ear, the child's pure, direct appreciation of music degenerates. If left to continue along that path, the child will be unable to hear the call of a bird or the sound of the wind as songs. That is why music education is thought to be beneficial to the child's development.

The child who is raised with an ear pure and clear may not be able to play the popular tunes on the violin or piano, but I do not think this has anything to do with the ability to hear true music or to sing. It is when the heart is filled with song that the child can be said to be musically gifted.

I think the Beatles are a very good musical education for children. All the family can love the Beatles. The younger ones love "Ob-La-Di, Ob-La-Da," "Octopus's Garden," "Here Comes the Sun" and "Yellow Submarine," while us adults love "Something" and "Across the Universe." And make songs up with your kids. It's surprisingly easy:

Mandy the cat is an elegant cat,
She loves to lie around.
Mandy the cat is a silent cat,
She never makes a sound.

There's an example for you of a little tune I made up with the kids.

So sing, parents, sing! Dance around the kitchen! Sing while you clean and cook and wash. Be joyful, be cheerful, cast resentment from your heart. Our singing confidence has been removed by the *American Idol* judge in our heads. "Oh, I can't sing!" we say. Well, I can't sing—I mean, I really can't sing—but I sing anyway. I have even stood on a stage in an Antwerp nightclub and sung "Seventeen" by the Sex Pistols to ukulele accompaniment in front of three hundred young Belgians.

One idea is to start a family jug band. All sorts of household implements can be used as percussion instruments, and elastic bands can be stretched over boxes to make twangy instruments. Perhaps someone can make a buzzing noise with a blade of grass.

I love dancing slowly round the kitchen table, children behind me, in the manner of that wonderful scene in Jim Jarmusch's film *Down by Law* where the three principal protagonists dance round their jail cell singing: "I scream, you scream, we all scream for ice cream!"

Music and dancing should be woven back into the fabric of everyday life. You don't have to be good at it to do it: your skill level doesn't matter. It is done for its own pleasure, and who cares if you're not the best? Music and dancing are the perfect ways to enjoy time with your kids: they are harmonizers, they bring you to the same level. They are not an adult imposition, nor does the adult resent doing it, which is certainly the case with some children's activities (playing on the swings, for example).

Sing all day, play music, dance. We have become too civilized, restrained, closed off. And go listen to the music of nature. How do you do that? We'll find out in the next chapter.

11.

End All Activities, Be Wild

Let the wild rumpus start!

MAURICE SENDAK, *Where the Wild Things Are*, 1963

Activities are the scourge of modern childhood. "Give them something to do": in that phrase you hear summed up our attitudes to childhood, and indeed life in general. Give them something to do, to keep them out of mischief. We have to give them something to do because we have made them incapable of finding things to do for themselves, the poor creatures. So we give them "something": anything, thing undefined, just a thing to keep them out of our hair. And finally, that word "do." It's a sickness of our culture, that "doing" is seen as superior to not doing, even if the "doing" might even cause harm.

The modern parent fills the child's day with enclosing activities. From the enclosure of school we enclose them in the car, and then we drive them to more adult-organized activities: ballet class, football, extra French, drama club, all in the service of making them into competitive entities. I hear that some Manhattan parents are even hiring Mandarin nannies so that their children can learn to speak Chinese, the better to compete in the global markets when they are older! Everywhere kids go, adults are right there, shepherding them around, tapping their behinds with sticks to ensure that they walk through the prearranged gates, monitoring, checking, controlling, measuring, protecting. Play is commodified: we take them to costly fun palaces, danger-free fun zones made of plastic, when right under our very noses places to play are freely available. I remember that the best places to play were old landfills, where we could find springs and fridges and old bits of cars. The best places were the places we had discovered for ourselves. We played in the margins. We didn't need adult-designed playgrounds. I remember even as a kid being keenly aware that there was something wrong with adult-organized fun. It was disabling.

In the house children resist the lovingly decorated playroom, the planned schemes. They play on the stairs, in the sitting room, in the hall. They move the furniture around and make dens. In the woods they build dens and little fantasy Robin Hood camps, away from the interfering gaze of adults. Let them play! Leave them alone! Let them take an old blanket and stretch it over two upturned chairs to make a roof. Let them build dams over streams. Let them make maps, burn matches and carry Swiss Army knives. The self-made places of play, the self-discovered zones: these are the best.

Remember the wise words of Hundertwasser, the Austrian

artist and architect: "As art cannot be taught and there are no human teachers, there are only two teachers, if you want a teacher at all: one is your own childhood, your own self; the other is nature."

We contort our lives to fit in with modern industrial clock tempos. All parents know how assiduously children resist being forced into punctuality: "How many times do I have to ask you? PUT YOUR SOCKS ON! We're going to be late." From an early age we train their spirits to be enclosed by time as if to prepare them for working nine-to-five shifts in a call center. By constant insistence we train them in the ethical value of punctuality. But they, by nature, escape from clock time and into the joy of simply being in the present moment whenever they have the chance.

Give them something to do! How many parents have ruined an afternoon with a well-intentioned drawing or painting or cooking session. All starts well. Mother and children—or father and children—spend twenty minutes or so happily creating together. It's wonderful to see the little ones using their hands, mixing ingredients together and slopping stuff around! The parent's vision of self-expressing tots is happily fulfilled. But then things start to go wrong. The kids mess around. They spill paint on their clothes or they paint their bodies. They throw things. The kids find this rupturing of the adult's carefully laid plans terrifically amusing. The parent does not, soon losing his or her temper and screaming, "Get out! Out! All of you!" and ending up icing the cookies or clearing the paints away all alone. The moral: Don't bother! Children can play very well if left alone.

Sporting activities present a problem for the idle parent. I remember being aghast when Victoria booked tennis lessons for Arthur, then aged five, every Saturday morning at nine. What sort of madness was that? Saturday mornings are for lying around doing nothing. Now, after five days of chaotic early mornings getting them ready for school, on Saturdays we finally have the chance to have tea in bed and stay there as long as possible while the kids wreck the house. But instead we voluntarily organize a load of expensive hassle, all because of some half-formed middle-class parental dream about creating a star tennis player. As luck would have it, after a few months Arthur decided he didn't want to continue with tennis lessons and so we knocked it on the head. Here's a tip: Don't let them get anywhere near the soccer team or the baseball team. You will find that your weekends are completely ruined by having to drive them to matches all over the place. Organized sports is the enemy. Skateboarding, yes. That is free, you can do it anywhere and there are no parents involved, or very few. But team sports? No, no, no.

That's not to mention early indoctrination into the pernicious creed of competition. There is something horribly Victorian about team sports. Somehow you are supposed to give up your individuality to a wider cause. And good team players are often unpleasant people: "Jock" is the expressive word for the type in some places. Team sports are all about beating the other team. They prepare young men for vicious competition in the workplace. But games don't have to be competitive, and any anthropologist will tell you that old-fashioned societies, which have more egalitarian systems of government, have their own games and sports but without the cutthroat Western competitive element.

Although I should add that I do not object in principle to learning how to swim—of course not, for as Locke wisely wrote:

> 'Tis that saves many a man's life: and the Romans thought it so necessary that they ranked it with letters; and it was the common phrase to mark one ill educated and good for nothing that he had neither learned to read nor swim. *Nec literas didicit nec natare.*

It's also fun. So swimming? Yes. But let's keep the adult-organized part of their lives down to a minimum.

Try not to fill children's days. Let them live. The idle parent tries to unite two things: the now and the future. We must try to enjoy our own daily lives while ensuring that our children are enjoying theirs. We want to give them a happy and free childhood. And we also want to ensure that they can look after themselves later, helping them to create their own lives, avoiding the stress, worry and ill health that so often result from operating in the conventional working world. Many overmothered men cling to the petticoats of a large corporation in later life (to steal a phrase from the anthropologist and *Continuum Concept* author Jean Liedloff). I want my children to be free, and I'd be happiest if they never got a job but found another way to earn a living. And even if they do follow a more conventional path, I hope they will do so with a free spirit and a lightness of touch. Too much activity will tend to make them dependent on outside authorities for the structure of their daily lives. Time is free; they should be given as much free time as possible, in order to feed their own imaginations and create self-reliance.

Children have a wild nature, as the best children's books acknowledge. For example, in *Where the Wild Things Are*, Max sails off to a parent-free world of wildness. Children want to go to the wild places, where they are free from authority and at liberty to create their own worlds. Some of my most vivid childhood memories are of playing games on hay bales or in the park or in trees. We need the smell of wood and leaves in our faces. However well intentioned, the adult's imposition of activity on the child may actually be a form of control: we have a preconceived idea of what we think the child should be doing and then we try to impose that vision (often with disastrous results because the children delight in disrupting our schemes).

If we overregulate, control and confine our children, we also run the risk of their wild spirit breaking free in some horrible, antisocial and destructive way. Think of joyriding, glue-sniffing, window-smashing, and car-scratching. The free spirit emerges somehow, sooner or later, like a bottled genie.

And what is the principle reason why we enclose our children? Fear. Fear of abduction, fear of pedophiles: "You can't be too careful these days" is the phrase I hear at the school gates. Yes, you can be too careful! We are all too careful! We have allowed stories of very rare abductions in the papers to make us think that this sort of thing happens all the time. It doesn't! There are something like a hundred abductions by strangers every year in the United States. The chance of an abduction is one in millions. The fear of the bogeyman is out of all proportion to the reality. It is newspapers and television news shows that create this fear. Because that is the very nature of the medium. Newspapers are cheap gossip sheets, purveyors of gossip in order to sell advertising: "Latest on the Ripper." They are vendors of salacious crime stories. When an abduction story appears in the papers, how the manufacturers of child restraint equipment must cheer. Sales up! Share price up! Happy investors! Rich board members, growing fat on fear!

But the system does not approve of wildness. In the UK, the Crime and Disorder Act (1998) gives the police the power to remove truanting kids from public places. One newspaper reported: "Ministers want to make it an offence to allow children to roam unsupervised in a public place." This idea of taming children has its roots in the Puritan attitude to small ones, which is more or less that they are wild and need the wildness knocking out of them. Here is the Protestant preacher Jonathan Edwards: "As innocent as children seem to be to us . . . [they] are young vipers, and are infinitely more hateful than vipers . . . they are naturally very senseless and stupid."

Such a view clearly justified the Puritans in the ferocious taming of their kids: "Break their will that you may save their souls," John Wesley would say. (They had similar attitudes, by the way, to the American Indians, whom they saw as barbarous, despite the fact that they had saved many early settlers from certain death.) So it was that discipline and factory work were introduced in order to tame the infant beast. One brainwashed eighteenth-century worker in a Massachusetts mill recalled of her childhood:

The discipline our work brought us was of great value. We were obliged to be in the mill at just such a minute, in every hour, in order to doff our full bobbins and replace them with empty ones. We went to our meals and returned at the same hour every day. We worked and played at regular intervals, and thus our hands became deft, our fingers nimble, our feet swift, and we were taught daily habits of regularity and industry; it was, in fact, a sort of manual training or industrial school.

Or just read Dickens to find out how that approach to things was later expressed in British schools and factories. When Victorian philanthropists finally began to raise objections to child labor they neatly introduced compulsory schooling to do the same job of accustoming children to rigid routine and long, boring days. State-funded education was introduced in 1833, in part to tame our children to the point where they would meekly submit to wage slavery.

Yet we crack down on wild behavior in the home from early in a child's life. For example, nudity is generally frowned on. *Idler* contributor Sarah Janes tells a wonderful story about how her nephew shocked his grandparents. The four-year-old boy was listening to music through headphones for the first time:

To see his enraptured face, tears twinkling in the corners of his eyes, his perfect body glowing with pleasure, was a sight I will never forget. The boy in his joy then started to take off his clothes, and the family tried to make him put them back on again. He wiggled his bare bottom at us, and then, not feeling sufficiently exposed—perhaps not making sufficient intimate contact with every joy-filled particle of air, he pulled apart his bum cheeks and showed us his arsehole. My mum and dad said: "That's enough now, Jack. That's not funny."

I'd noticed my own children doing precisely this. Before I read Sarah's piece I'd been tempted, like Joyce Grenfell, to say: "Henry—don't do that." But after reading it I thought, who cares? If we tell them off for being joyful, the little Jacks will learn to hide and conceal both their joy-filled arseholes and their own wild spirits. We tame, repress and smother our children. Again, it's a post-Industrial obsession. Look at medieval cathedrals and you will find bare bottoms and exposed genitals peeping from the pillars and buttresses. A corbel at the church of Notre Dame des Miracles in Mauriac has a carving of a naked female contortionist with her arsehole and vagina opened wide. A carving on the church of St. Pierre at Champignolles has a man showing his buttocks. There is a wonderful arsehole in the courtyard of the Hostal de los Reyes Católicos in Santiago de Compostela. And that is not to mention the many medieval church carvings of men and women having sex. Such architectural features would be unthinkable today, so prudish we have become, on any building, let alone a church. And yet we consider ourselves to be so liberated! Clearly one hundred years of Victorian prudishness has damaged our psyches, bar the occasional coach of football fans, exposing their bottoms in the window on the highway. Maybe things have improved slightly since the 1950s, when schools commonly banned masturbation, according to A. S. Neill. But it appears to me that we are nowhere near as freethinking as we like to believe, and to congratulate ourselves for our supposed freedom is simultaneously hubristic and stupid.

The great ordering and taming of the world, which covered up a new brutality and willingness to exploit, began in the fifteenth century and is still going on today. Medieval childhood was far less strictly supervised, controlled and regulated than modern childhood. But on the other hand, there existed all sorts of educational establishments and indeed many of today's universities were founded in the Middle Ages. Medieval doctors adopted the Roman idea of dividing childhood into three stages: *infantia*— birth to age seven; *pueritia*—seven to twelve for girls and seven to fourteen for boys; and *adolescentia*—twelve or fourteen to twenty-one. Medieval people were very careful about small babies: in fourteenth-century child-care manuals, mothers are advised to bathe the child every morning and play with it.

Children started working earlier, and this may have been no bad thing: lads and lasses like to be useful and to contribute. School actually prevents children from contributing to society. It separates them. It is also true that there were far fewer books on child-molding. It hadn't yet occurred to the moralists that children could be objects of experiment for moral training. Locke says that he wrote *Some Thoughts* for a particular gentleman's son, who "being then very little, I considered only as white paper or wax, to be moulded and fashioned as one pleases."

Respect the child, for each is unique and different. Help your child to follow its own course. I am not saying that you should indulge bad behavior. You have to have some rules, otherwise they will mess up your house. No boots in the house is one of ours. But we give the rule not as part of the child's moral instruction but simply as a practical and personal matter: I do not want to have to clean up their mud. Our rules are subjective, not objective. We do not hold up some higher authority, or say "that is bad." Better than "that is bad" is to say, "I don't like that." A. S. Neill says that he would shout at a child for walking into his study with muddy boots on. But that is different from having a cold hard rule that is punished coldly. Personally, I think screaming and losing one's temper, while certainly to be avoided, is preferable to a calm telling-off, along the lines of: "You have done wrong. And now I'm going to punish you." With the former, you remain a human being. With the latter, you are attempting to act as some kind of higher power, an Old Testament Yahweh.

Fear not the wild spirit. I remember when the noted heavy-metal band Zodiac Mindwarp and the Love Reaction played a gig in our barn. An eight-year-old and a ten-year-old in the audience completely lost themselves to the music: they were jumping up and down, banging their heads, staring wildly, rocking out! I have seen similar primal expressions on boys' faces when gathered around the bonfire. "Boys love a bonfire," as William Cobbett observes in his pig-killing chapter in *Cottage Economy*. A bonfire allows the primal spirit to be expressed. It is a connection with nature. It can also encourage a meditative gazing. I suppose bonfires will be outlawed next, on health and safety grounds.

I should add also that I think men and women need the occasional Dionysian orgy. A blow-off a couple of times a year is important for parents. Dump the kids on your parents for three days. Put on the Detroit techno, intoxicate yourselves and dance all night. Parents are apt to become overserious after their children are born. But we need to treat life as a dance, not as a trial, not as hard work.

We should fill our own worlds and the worlds of our children with pleasures. These need not be costly, and for what it's worth, here are a few practical suggestions from me. But of course, once your mind starts to work in this way, you will come up with your own ideas.

(a) Build Fires

Make fires as often as you can. Burn stuff. Not barbecues, those prim, polite, enclosed suburban fire substitutes, but real fires. Make a fire pit in the garden and surround it with stones. Fill it with household paper and cardboard. Pick up sticks or bits of wood from skips or from the park. A bonfire after school is so much more fun than telly and computer games. Arthur's idea of heaven is toasting marshmallows on the fire. And it's something that parents enjoy, too, because, after all, they need to be connected to the primal a lot more often as well. Dads in particular enjoy fires. And perhaps you could get a big cooking pot and hang it over the fire on a tripod and cook and eat outdoors. A good fire will last until the morning, doubling the pleasure: before school (assuming that, unlike us, you will have the time) show them how to scrape away the top layer of ashes to reveal the hot embers smoldering below, hot enough to relight the half-burned twigs that are lying around and get the fire going again.

(b) Get Out

Some of my happiest childhood memories are of weekends spent in the large gardens of my parents' friends' house, where we played without supervision but near enough the house to run back and find someone if things went wrong. When older we would spend hours in Richmond Park. My father used to take us for days out there when we were smaller, with a camping stove to fry sausages—such intense pleasure. And as we grew, we came to know the park so well that we could safely go alone. Now things are even better: when the kids are asleep, the parents can have sex in the woods. Reconnect to the Green Man within.

(c) Sofa Games

Why get up? It's amazing how much fun you can have with your kids without leaving the sofa. I've already mentioned Tickle or Trap. You can also fend off attackers. The kids can run around the room while you try to trip them up or grab them. They can throw balls at you. They can climb all over you. I've often thought that it would be fun to see how long you could play with them while remaining on the sofa.

(d) Wrestling Time

This, though I say so myself, has been a great success. We now do it every evening after supper. My motivation was that the boys, in particular, seemed to have an abundance of pent-up energy, which was being expressed in unhelpful ways, such as screaming and tantrums and generally smashing things up. But wrestling is also great fun, for kids and for Dad, and leaves Mom free to do some jobs without being hassled. It's me against them. The three children stand on one corner of the rug in the sitting room, with me at the other corner. I say: "Round One, three, two, one," and then Henry says, "Ding ding." We then prowl around one another in the ring. I lock arms with Arthur, making growling noises, and then hurl him in the air. The other two jump on my back, like little monkeys trying to bring down a bear. The game is either that I hold all three of them for ten seconds, in which case I have won that round, or they hold me down for ten seconds. We do three rounds (and that's enough for me). The children absolutely love it. Henry wants to do it all day: "Daddy, can we do Wessling Time?" he asks me while I'm working. It's just really good to holler and shout, and to watch their faces flush red with excitement. It tires them out and I hope provides an outlet for the wild thing within.

12.

No More Family Days Out

He who binds to himself a joy
Does the winged life destroy;
But he who kisses the joy as it flies
Lives in eternity's sun rise.

WILLIAM BLAKE, "Eternity"

There can be no more absurd invention of modern industrial society than the family day out. All week you have been stressed out at work, as you have tried to conform to someone else's idea of who you should be. You are tired, grumpy and guilty because you have hardly seen your children. It's time, you reflect, to give the kids a treat, do something together. I know! Let's chase some fun! Let's pile everyone into the car and join all the other desperate families at the local theme park! We can spend a pile of cash there and everything will be all right again.

The trouble starts with the inexpressible headache of getting everybody out of the house. Before children, I used to just stroll out of the house. Now this process cannot be achieved without an hour of screaming, searching for lost socks and shoes, huffing, puffing, shouting, cursing Britax and their cruel inventions in the name of child safety. (Those accursed car seats might restrain the child, but they do a huge amount of psychic damage to the father, not to mention causing him physical pain as he tries to get the seat belts in their slots.) Then you have to find various toys that the children seem to find completely indispensable for the journey. Recently we made the terrible mistake of installing one of those DVD players in the back of the car, in the hope that it would keep the kids quiet on long journeys. It can help, I suppose, but the darned thing never seems to work properly, and fixing it is yet another task to add to the interminable torture of leaving the house. (And what was wrong with "I Spy" and daydreaming?)

Then the real hell begins.

We start to drive to the theme park. They fight. "Lila hit me!" "Henry bit me! On purpose." "Arthur head-butted me!" The three children, tightly bound in the back of the car, start lashing out at each other. Each child has perfected their own uniquely irritating crying noise. Delilah's is a sort of constant mosquito whine mixed with helpless sobbing that apparently prevents her from being able to articulate the nature of her complaint. Arthur wails as if the world is about to end and it's all so unfair and un-just. And Henry makes the sort of noises that the makers of *The Exorcist* would have been proud to feature in the movie. Both mother and father now start shouting. Mother wheels round and screams: "How many times do I have to tell you? Leave him alone!" Dad bellows: "Right, Arthur, one more time and there's no ice cream. I mean it."

Dad anxiously glances in the rearview mirror to see what's going on. For a while I congratulate myself for not losing my temper. Then I suddenly break. I have been known to go berserk, to swear and bang the windscreen in my rage. Then, if I lose my temper, Victoria takes this as her cue to seize the moral high ground and say something like "We're fed up with you," thus driving me into a deeper rage, which cannot really be expressed well since we're all trapped in this blessed car. Every second we are burning up oil, and the price of gas seems to shoot up every day. (The average cost of keeping a car is supposed to be around $8,000 a year and rapidly rising: imagine how many taxis you could get for that? Do we really need our cars? Certainly it would make sense to use them a lot less. Staying at home instead of going on a family day out is the green answer too: no resources used up and no expense! Create a good life on a low income and you will be in a very powerful position: at no other man's beck and call, able to laugh at big business and government.)

Soon you arrive at the theme park, and a sense of being conned overwhelms you. You are being ripped off, commodified, victimized, your weakness profited from. This is the slaves' day off. But should fun really have to be paid for? Idle parenting is low-cost parenting. We need to avoid the spending of money at all times.

Next comes the ferocious boredom of queueing up for rides, while idly speculating about the other families around you. Are they happy? Do they also go home to door slammings, screamings and grumpiness? The theme park is a strangely lonely place. Hundreds mill past each other but rarely speak, like mute zombie families. Lunch is an overpriced, prepackaged nightmare. Time drags on: it's only two o'clock. How much longer before I can get out of this hellhole? The children constantly demand more rides. At the end of the day you go to the gift shop, cunningly placed at the exit, and you say "no" a thousand times. Here we see the paradox of plenty: shopping actually means not shopping, because for every one thing you buy you have said "no" to a thousand others. Far from being an exercise in indulgence, shopping is all about limiting yourself: I can only afford so much. So however generous you allow yourself to be, in actual fact you use all your energy preventing the children from buying more. So shopping has disappointment built into it. The child is full of frustration because he has glimpsed forbidden delights: imagine what his parents could have bought him if they weren't so mean or poor.

The same goes for museums as for theme parks. I took Arthur to the Natural History Museum recently, and found the experience to be, in the word much favored by William Morris to describe the low-quality output of industrial society, "shoddy." Shoddy exhibits, shoddy design and decoration, silly little walkways that diminish the splendor of the rooms. And there is the same suffocating feeling of containment as at the theme park: the same stifling restriction on movement, with gates and turnstiles and preprepared routes to be shuffled along obediently. I feel lost in those places.

Also, why is it that only my children seem to be so naughty

on days out? Everyone else's seem the picture of restraint. But rest assured, every parent is going through the same agonies. If only we'd just taken them to a field! Life could be so much simpler.

Then the hell of the drive home. Now the children and the parents are cross and fidgety. The children always want to stay longer than the parents—"We're going now." "Owwwww! Why? Why? Why?" Most likely the children are coming down off a junkfood sugar rush. In the back of the car, they kick, pull each other's hair and snatch each other's new toys. The threat to abandon them in a rest area does not seem to help matters. Even after I stop the car, they continue fighting. We've noticed that the best policy, although very difficult to carry out, is simply to ignore them. I remember one journey when V and I were simply too tired to tell them off. We couldn't be bothered. They had a fight in the back, and then, miraculously, stopped arguing, without any intervention from the authorities. Probably we intervene far too much. In any case, I always find it impossible to work out who started it, who was in the right, who was in the wrong. I try to act as impartial judge and always fail. Their individual cases always sound so convincing. At last, at home, I say: "Okay, I'm leaving the room. I'll be back in three minutes. You can sort it out among yourselves." Amazingly, this works.

After supper, during which the children will probably have behaved appallingly, they have to be bathed and put to bed. The evening promises a couple of hours of exhausted drinking before you collapse into bed at half past ten, poor and disappointed.

This is not the idle way.

The truly idle delight instead in staying at home. At home you are free. You can create your own fun, at no cost whatsoever. You can let the children run around while you read a book. There is a world of adventure and learning under your own roof and on your own doorstep. We often now stay at home all day on Saturday and all day on Sunday. We play in the kitchen. We make food together. One happy day I sat in the armchair reading my William Morris biography while Henry played on the floor with his toy tractors, Delilah cut up bits of paper and Arthur read *The Beano*. Later I found myself making a pair of sunglasses out of a cereal packet with Delilah. Children love making things, playing, being busy. They love creating their own fun. People are scared to stay at home all day because they think the kids will get bored. We seek external stimulus and we don't understand that each one of us has a huge, untapped store of creativity. But *things happen of their own accord*. You don't need to leave the house. We think we are enjoying ourselves at the theme park, but really it's a disabling sort of fun because it's passive. It actually follows the familiar pattern of twenty-first-century life: long periods of boredom interspersed with the occasional thrill. And we don't have to make any effort beyond getting out our wallets. The rides, in return for cash, hurl us around in a parody of real pleasure. At home you can play Scrabble, you can eat on the floor, the kids can make dens. You can learn how to play together, or you can get on with your own jobs and pleasures and let the children exist around you. And you don't even have to bother to play with them.

My friend James doesn't play with his son. I asked him to explain himself:

> Fertile neglect is the name of that policy: leaving the boy to his own devices so I can pursue mine and he can develop those solitary skills that will serve him in future airports, waiting rooms and prisons. It came about simply because I found actual down-at-his-level waving-tiny-figurines PLAYING to be, for some reason, soul-destroying—the arbitrary and despotic movements of the child-mind and all that. Bonus side effect: when you do consent, in moments of magnanimity, to lower yourself to their play-level they are incredibly grateful.

Now when it comes to museums, I should add that the country is full of eccentric little museums that have more charm and interest than the big ones, should you want to relax your no-days-out policy and search out the small rather than the obvious. For example, the other day I discovered, simply by aimlessly wandering, a wonderful museum of curios in Gower Street in London called the Grant Museum. It has 55,000 specimens crowded into a basement room. There you have elephant skulls and frogs in jars. It is completely empty of people, and everything is arranged in a charming higgledypiggledy fashion, like a Victorian gentleman explorer's private collection. And no gift shop at the end!

Or you could make your own museum of artifacts. One idea I had was for a Chamber of Horrors. I placed a few awful Christmas presents on the wall, like the tie decorated with Day-Glo mushrooms that my dad once gave me, held up a candle to each in turn and screamed with horror. Put some things on a shelf. Buy a butterfly net. There is natural history everywhere, not just in a London museum. Remember the words of Nabokov: "My pleasures are the most intense known to man: writing and butterfly hunting." Instead of driving to a fun park, build a tree house. We built ours, largely from stuff lying around, for eighty bucks. Explore your own street, your own garden, your own house. There is a wonderful fund of pleasure and enjoyment there for the taking and you need look no further than between your own two ears. Your own home can be full of adventure, and to ensure that your adult sensibilities remain stimulated and to guard against the ever present danger of becoming a resentment-filled slave to your children, also keep a good book on the go—poetry, essays, a novel. Short novels are good; short stories are very good.

You can also use time with the children to learn things yourself. Now is the time to teach yourself to draw. Draw with them. Learn to draw animals by copying from books. I taught myself how to draw a simple crab and simple lobster while on holiday in Cornwall. Once you have reduced animal drawing to a few basics, you can then teach the kids and they'll be mighty pleased with their own results. We give too much responsibility for learning and being creative to the schools. We must learn and teach at home. This need not be a trial, but can be a great joy for parent and child. But you must always make sure that you are genuinely enjoying yourself. Doing things for other people's sake will lead to feelings of corrosive resentment that will then find expression in some unhealthy fashion, like cancer. Your first responsibility is to your own happiness. If you are unhappy and you do things merely out of a sense of duty rather than genuine love and generosity, then others will sense that and ugliness will result. When the children get home from school, be already sitting at the kitchen table—not fussing about with washing up. Set a good idling example.

My other important piece of advice when it comes to family days out is: *split up*. Any combination of family members—any—is easier, we find, than the five of us squeezed together in the metal box. In fact, any other combination tends to be a joy. I would far rather take the three of them on my own somewhere than go with all five of us. On my own, things can be easier: I do what I want. There is no one to argue with and no one to shuffle responsibility on to: the responsibility is all yours. This also has the added bonus of giving Victoria a break. For this reason, I am happy to look after the kids alone for three days, if V needs a rest or wants to go to visit friends. In some ways it's easier, because you give yourself up to the task fully, without half hoping that the other person is going to do the work. Then I can have three days alone at some other point. Constant breaks from each other are essential.

Or split into two parties. I find that once removed from the structure of the familiar nuclear family my children behave beautifully. Things have their own natures, and the nature of the nuclear family is to be conflict-filled. Perhaps the kids behave better when removed from this institution because outside it they are individuals who are accorded respect rather than simply being family members expected to play out their customary dysfunctional roles.

I took Arthur on his own to see his granny, and we had a wonderful day out. You will accuse me of betraying my principles, but we even went to that fun zone Brighton Pier.

Once I recovered from my very deep disappointment at the fact that there is no longer a single pinball machine on Brighton Pier, only those cascade machines where coins pile up tantalizingly close to you, always about to tumble down, we ate ice cream and went on the fun-fair rides at the end of the pier, and later we found the Penny Arcade with all the old-fashioned 1920s slot machines. Old technology is so much more charming than the new, and the Penny Arcade was clearly a labor of love for its owner, in contrast to the well-organized banditry of the pier. Arthur said later that this was his favorite part of the whole day. No whining or arguing! Bliss to spend time with him in that way, bliss. And it's the same with the others: now that we have three children, to be with only one or two of them seems like an absolute breeze. So I implore you, split up! Life will become so much easier. Split them up, stay at home, explore your own backyard or send your partner away for the weekend. Hang out, in that wonderful American phrase. Don't do things. Let things happen. Just sit one day around the table, start talking and see what happens. You will be amazed at all the wonderful ideas that come out of the children's minds, and amazed at the creativity that you will find in yourself if you simply stop and listen. The idea of the happy family, those (always young, beautiful and smiling manically) families in ads for holidays: it's pure myth.

But happiness is not impossible. It would be nice if, when

grown up, your kids said to their friends: "I had a happy child-hood." That is worth more than all the expensive family days out, holidays, toys, high grades at school or sporting achieve-ments. Try to ensure that your children are enjoying their every-day life—and the best way to do that is to find that positive negligence, a sort of yay-saying respect, to leave them alone but also to be there when you're needed. Don't worry about the future. Enjoy your life with them now. Set them free.

I should also warn against perfectionism when it comes to home interiors, particularly when there are small children about. You can put a lot of work and thought and money into some inte-rior development, only to have it all ruined by the pesky kids. We have decided not to bother making the house neat while they are growing up (it's a convenient philosophy for the idle parent, be-cause it also excuses us a lot of work). About three years ago we decorated, and two days later the children drew big swirly patterns and crosses on the walls and doors with ballpoint pens. I was furi-ous, livid. But now there is writing all over their bedroom walls. And I think: good. That's one more room we don't have to worry about. Give up. There will be plenty of time to create your beauti-ful house as you grow older. Give up on creating the ideal home and instead embrace the idle home. No more poring through in-teriors magazines and feeling inferior ("World of Inferiors" was my friend Gavin Hills's gag). No more expense and no more worry. We have learned to love the woodchip. This isn't to say you must give up on style all together, but whitewashed walls, hung with pictures, and a geranium will go a long way. Keep the furniture to a minimum. We recently removed the broken old chairs from the kitchen and installed two benches that I found lying around in the village hall storeroom. The bench instantly declutters the kitchen, and it also has a pleasingly medieval vibe. I like the medieval interior, a few pieces of simple wooden furniture. A chest. Plain walls but with fabrics draped around the place.

13.

How to Enjoy Mealtimes, with Some Thoughts on Manners

People should think less about what they ought to do
and more about what they ought to be.

Meister Eckhart (1260–1327)

F amily mealtimes can be a trial. There is the fidgety writhing of the eight-year-old boy who seems incapable of sitting still. He has ants in his pants. There is the wild three-year-old who flings food around the room and drops it in his glass of water. And there is the self-pitying whine of the six-year-old girl: "Henry's got the stripy bowl. I never, *ever* get the stripy bowl." How did we create such horrors, and why do they behave so badly? And why do we get so angry with them? Do we really care that much about table manners? Perhaps those families we hear about who never sit down to eat together but stuff themselves with TV dinners on the sofa have got it right. Why do we parents put ourselves through the hell of it? Well, it's because mealtimes together, sharing food, can be a huge pleasure. Dad can give vent to the full range of his dry humor. The children can laugh together, and Mother or Father can take pleasure in the preparation of food. And we idle parents want to resist the atomization of eating, where everyone eats something different, even in different rooms. The idle parent at all times wants to harmonize, not separate.

Let's look at manners first. It was the conviction of A. S. Neill that we all get ourselves in too much of a bother about mealtime manners. His experience was that kids learn good manners naturally as they grow older, and from example rather than authority. Certainly we all know that our children tend to behave better in their friends' houses than when they are at home.

Neill makes a distinction between good manners and mere etiquette. Manners he sees as a natural result of a calm and generous soul: "Manners cannot be taught, for they belong to the unconscious." Etiquette, he says, "is the veneer of manners." "Artificial manners are the first layer of hypocritical veneer to be dropped under freedom . . . in Summerhill we ask for no manners at all, not even a 'thank you' or a 'please.' Yet again and again, visitors say, 'But their manners are delightful!'"

I agree with Neill in theory. There is something unpleasant about the hovering parent, who is always there prompting the child ("What do you say?") when it is given something. The child will smirk and mumble, "Thank you." But in practice, though, it's not so easy: I've tried to ignore bad manners, but I tend to fall at the first hurdle. When I see Arthur writhing at the table, apparently unable to use knife and fork, stuffing his mouth with his fingers, I confess that my inner Puritan loses its temper.

We all seem to behave badly at home. Today, for example, I hang my head in shame because I threw a pair of boots at Arthur and they hit him. He had been complaining and asked me to carry him from the car to the house rather than undergo the inconvenience of putting on his boots and walking himself. So I lost my temper, furious at his wimpiness. When V saw his muddy face she was furious with me, rightly. And anyway, who has bred this lack of fortitude in him? I have only myself to blame. We must concentrate on our own pleasure in simply being rather than try to change the outward actions of those around us.

We all do appalling things and perhaps we parents need to improve our own manners, toward the children and toward our partners, before imposing courtesy through force of authority. After all, if the children see the parents behaving with a lack of respect to each other, then they will surely follow suit? Can we *demand* manners and respect from our children? Neill thinks not: "When a person really gives respect, he does so unawares. My pupils can call me a silly ass any time they like to; they respect me because I respect their young lives. . . . My pupils and I have mutual respect for each other because we approve of each other."

In former times, and in old-fashioned cultures today, courtesy was insisted upon from a young age. There are wonderful guides to table manners from the medieval era:

Have not too many words, from swearing keep aloof, For all such manners come to an evil proof.

So goes one couplet from a late medieval poem called "How the Good Wife Taught Her Daughter." Similarly in *The Romance of the Rose* we find a disquisition on table manners aimed at the lady of the house:

> She should not take one long-breathed draft, Whether from cup or hanap quaffed, But gently taste with sipping soft Now and again, but not too oft . . .

In the thirteenth century, elegance of manners was an important part of social harmony, and while I agree with Neill's arguments on manners in general, I make an exception when it comes to table manners and come down on the side of the medieval etiquette writers. Certainly we could benefit from the reinjection of ritual into mealtimes. Nowadays we all fall on our food as it is put in front of us, with no saying of grace or even the faintest suggestion of a ritual. Ritual is good because it slows us down and creates a little space for reflection. We need to make time for meals. Less television, longer periods sitting at table.

What really drives me and Victoria crazy at home is the kids' fussiness over food. After Victoria has spent an hour preparing them a range of delicious dishes, it is terribly disheartening—nay, enraging—to hear our spoiled little Western kids saying:

> "It's dis-*gus*-ting."
> "Yuck!" (followed by a dramatic spitting out and reaching for the water glass)
> "I *hate* cauliflower/broccoli/raisins/potatoes/pasta/fish pie."

Yes, their tedious lists of likes and dislikes. "What makes you think we're interested?" asks my friend Alice when the kids start reeling off their lists of preferences. It is perhaps because they have such little control over other areas of their lives, so over-regulated are they, that in this one small area they revel in exercising their lordliness. Perhaps, also, we have given them too much choice in the matter. We are always asking them if they would *like* something, rather than just giving it to them. I think again the answer may be to go back to a medieval approach. Give them each an empty plate (or better, a piece of bread—less washing up!) and place the food down the middle of the table, cut into small pieces. Then let them grab away with fingers, a sort of tapas arrangement. Provide rose-scented bowls of water for cleaning the fingers. Perhaps it's the British habit of piling up a huge plateful of preapproved components that our kids object to. It simply looks too daunting—and it has been imposed by an authority, so what better way to state one's own desire for independence than to reject what's been offered?

Think how we hover about them and encourage the development of likes and dislikes when they are little, and the disastrous results: "Some water? No, not water? Some juice, perhaps? Apple? No? Orange, then. In the blue cup? The red cup, then. Please don't throw it on the floor. Henry, if you do that again, you'll be out. Henry, did you hear what I said?" and so on.

At home we have become somewhat mean and ascetic, partly because it simply makes life easier. We put a jug of water on the table, no juice or milk. They get used to it quickly enough. My aim is to create a sort of Dotheboys Hall in the kitchen: the family lined up neatly on our benches, gratefully eating and drinking whatever is put in front of them. Water, porridge, bread: that's it!

We should try to keep the food simple. If we don't put so much effort into cooking for them, then we won't be too disappointed when they whine "I don't li-i-i-ke it." I tend to feed the children baked beans on toast when I am alone. I know they like it and it's easy to make. And although we never have ready meals, I do think we could make the occasional exception and keep a few pizzas in the freezer, for those times when you can't be bothered to cook a proper meal.

Simplicity and good bread: this was the solution recommended by Locke. This would be proper home-baked bread, though, not that cottonwool stuff from the factory. He advises a largely vegetarian diet for the small ones: "Flesh should be forborne, as long as he is in [petti]coats, or at least till he is two or three years old."

For breakfast, Locke suggests porridge, "very sparingly seasoned with sugar, or rather none at all." Oatmeal, I understand, is what they call a super-food, and we find that our kids like it very much, especially as we give them maple syrup with it. It uses no milk and is very cheap. We buy the wholesale oats in twenty-pound sacks. No breakfast cereals. Locke is also a great fan of brown bread: "I should think that a good piece of well-made and well-baked brown bread, sometimes with and sometimes without butter or cheese, would be often the best breakfast for my young master."

Well, that's easily arranged. Rather than a choice of five breakfast cereals (are we running a B&B here?), let them have just porridge and bread. If you fancy it, cook some good bacon and eggs too. You see how easy it is to provide the sort of life that the seventeenth century's finest philosopher recommends for his young gentleman?

And now here's a surprise from the ever practical Locke: he is against regular mealtimes! He says we should shift the times and feed children lots of snacks:

> As to his meals, I should think it best that, as much as it can be conveniently avoided, they should not be kept constantly to an hour: for when custom has fixed his eating to certain stated periods, his stomach will expect victuals at the usual hour, and grow peevish if he passes it; either fretting itself into a trouble-some excess, or flagging into a downright want of appetite. Therefore I would have no time kept constantly to for his breakfast, dinner and supper, but rather varied almost every day. And if between these, which I call meals, he will eat, let him have, as often as he calls for it, good dry bread.

I find this piece of advice liberating. Too often baby-care and child-care manuals put forward strict prescriptions for precise timings of meals. But it is precisely a too-rigid adherence to clock time that can cause the difficulties. Clock time acts as a sort of abstract authority figure in our heads, "ticking us off," as the writer Jay Griffiths puts it. We get behind schedule and then we scream at our kids for dawdling, when all they are really doing is expressing their natural urge to enjoy the moment. So to reject clock time, at least partially and whenever possible, in the happy anarchy of the idle parent's home, would seem to be an excellent scheme.

We now turn to the vital topic of talking while eating. I have read that both the Yequana Indians and the families of Lark Rise in Flora Thompson's account of 1880s rural life took their meals more or less in silence. While this may occasionally seem attractive, I confess that in fact we like a good deal of noise and laughter at table. Mealtimes are great for telling funny stories and jokes. Make the experience of eating together enjoyable and the kids will look forward to it. Mealtimes are an opportunity to teach children how to talk and also how to listen, and that means not interrupting. It appears that in the seventeenth century as much as today kids had little interest in the idea of waiting their turn to speak:

> There is a sort of unmannerliness very apt to grow with young people, if not early restrained, and that is a forwardness to interrupt others that are speaking, and to stop them with some contradiction. . . . There cannot be a greater rudeness than to interrupt another in the current of his discourse. . . . Young men should be taught not to be forward to interpose their opinions unless asked or when others have done and are silent, and then only by way of inquiry not instruction. . . . Frequent interruptions in arguing, and loud wrangling, are too often observable amongst grown people, even of rank, amongst us.

Clearly this is a personal bugbear of Locke's. But it is hard to disagree. Locke then continues, rather in the manner of a contemporary radical anthropologist, to hold up the example of the native culture of the Americas, as evidence that there may be a better way of doing things: "The Indians, who we call barbarous, observe much more decency and civility in their discourses and conversation, giving one another a fair silent hearing till they have quite done and then answering them calmly and without noise or passion."

Somehow, in conversation as in business, the civilized world has introduced conflict rather than harmony as a guiding principle. I'm sure Locke would have been shocked by the rudeness of some of our contemporary radio interviewers and their subjects. Another point of manners that we try to insist on is for the child to look an adult in the eye when being spoken to. I can't bear that shuffling, ground-staring thing that kids do.

If children have a natural built-in sense of dignity and a resistance to authority, then when it comes to food it makes sense to involve them in its preparation. Then they are less likely to turn up their noses at the results. I would recommend much bread-baking at home, as it is work that can be shared by everyone. Making bread is an enjoyable and satisfying activity, and even three-year-olds can help with the kneading. Henry makes his own little loaves, which, of course, he loves to eat. And children can also be encouraged to add their own ingredients to the mix: raisins, nuts, oats, seeds, bits of Terry's Chocolate Orange—whatever is lying around. Then they have made their own unique bread. They can name it: Arthur's Wonder Bread. And they can decorate the loaves or buns.

We need to do things together and to break down the distinction between work and domestic life. I would love the kids not even to recognize a difference between work and play: imagine if they could enjoy doing the dishes as much as going to the cinema! This is surely possible. I am currently attempting to involve the entire family in cleaning up: I wash, the younger two dry, and the eldest puts away. It's easiest with our three-year-old because no one has yet told him that it's unpleasant. All activity is the same to him: a game. He has not yet learned how to discriminate and rank. It's not always easy with the other two. Arthur—how he dawdles! And then how tempted I am to bellow. He doesn't seem to mind, though, as he is busy making it all into a game as well, inventing little systems with string and pulleys. This all started when—oh, happy day!—the dishwasher broke. I'd been campaigning against this ugly whirring power-drainer for years. The dishwasher wrecks the idea of the family's doing the dishes together. Because the parents have to unload it. When we all work together, the whole job, including putting away, is done in about fifteen minutes. It's not always easy to get them started—indeed, they resist being told what to do—but once we have begun, it can even be enjoyable: many hands make light work—and you can listen to music or sing songs while you are doing it.

I was pondering the reason why Arthur resists helping with doing the dishes so forcefully. I concluded that it was because he had seen or heard us complaining about it ourselves and therefore learned that it is a despised activity of low status. So I resolved to at least put on an appearance of enjoying the chore, singing while working, with the idea that the kids would be fooled into thinking that it's something enjoyable. This trick could apply to any form of work: whistle and pretend to enjoy it when there are kids around. This way you can train them to work for you.

Growing your own fruit and vegetables together is another easy way to encourage the kids to enjoy good food. Start at the planning stage by asking them what they would like to grow. Peas are the wonder-crop here. "You can never have enough peas," wrote the great farmer John Seymour, and he was dead right. Eaten straight from the pod, they have all the fun value of cheese dip with a zillion times the nutritional value. They come in a compostable wrapping! And their small size makes them ideal for kids. And they are very tasty, almost unbelievably sweet. Kids enjoy puttering in the kitchen, while eating the odd one or many. And they can eat as many as they like. Peas are our most ancient vegetable. This year I am going to sow three times as many peas as last year. It is very easy: you don't need well-rotted compost for them. You simply dig a ditch under where they are going to be sown, and then chuck in fresh kitchen waste. Add a layer of soil, sow the peas and then cover with more soil. I use Kelvedon Wonder seeds and the tall-growing Alderman peas. Protect them, though, from birds. My hens wrecked many of my best-laid pea plans with their pecking and dirt bathing. Our other favorite is the French climbing bean, long purple pods that turn green on cooking, in satisfying Willy Wonka fashion. The more you can grow at home and the more you can indulge your children, the better. They will like vegetables and they will know where they came from. It's also cheaper than buying vegetables and gardening is a free activity for the kids: it doesn't bear comparison with the costly waste of a day out to the theme park. They will learn far more, too, when gardening. Take them with you when you go to the vegetable patch and let them hunt for slugs in return for hard cash, or make bug traps or lists of wildlife, or sow seeds, which they will do in delightfully carefree fashion. Henry especially enjoys carting muck with his mini wheelbarrow.

So make food at home, and try to grow it. Let the kids make bread and cake. Relearn the arts of life alongside the children. And encourage good manners, ideally by example, but if that doesn't work, by *brute force!*

14.

Let Animals Work for You

For a man to be trustworthy . . . the boy must have been in the
habit of being kind and considerate toward animals; and nothing
is so likely to give him that excellent habit as his seeing from his
very birth, animals taken great care of, and treated with
great kindness by his parents, and now-and-then
having a little thing to call his own.

WILLIAM COBBETT, *Cottage Economy*, 1823

don't like mud!" screams my mother on the rare occasions she
comes to visit us down on the farm. "I don't like it. And why
have you got all these animals?" My mother's philosophical approach to the world could be defined as "anti-nature enlightenment." She believes in the power of hard work and ingenuity to
replace mud, and chickens wandering through the kitchen, and
cold and wet, and all the awkward messes of nature with paving
stones and supermarkets and central heating. She likes clean,

tidy, mud-free spaces. She wants to conquer nature. She lives in a world of shining chrome and gleaming white plastic kitchen appliances. And she hates animals. We never had a cat or a dog when I was growing up. I was allowed a hamster, Toby. And a second one, a nervous little creature called Claude. After Claude we had a free-range gerbil called Kevin, who lived behind the kitchen units and whose short but exciting life came to an end when my father trod on him. "He ran under my foot," was how my dad put it.

So when we moved to our scruffy farmhouse I at last had the freedom to get some proper animals involved in our lives. The first additions were Milly and Mandy, two tortoiseshell cats, now aged five. These two sisters have suffered an enormous amount of abuse from our children over the years. They have been hurled from a first-floor window. They have had their tails cruelly pulled. Milly on one occasion was suspended in midair by her tail. They have been squashed, sat on, chased. But what is wonderful is how little they have retaliated. Animals seem to sense when their attacker is a mere child and is not posing a serious threat, so they don't scratch or bite. Only once or twice have the cats given the children a little warning snap of the teeth, when they have been pushed beyond endurance. Indeed, I have often found myself willing the animals to make a more decisive attack, in order to end the teasing and teach the children a lesson.

It's true, though, that the cats produce some pretty dreadful smells. Finding sloppy cat turds under my desk in the morning is not a pleasant way to start the day. And sometimes we simply cannot find the source of the stink. I have been known to ascend into apocalyptic rages when discovering cat messes around the house.

"They're coming *in* to have a shit!" I scream. We throw them out at every opportunity, with the result that they mew piteously at my study window in the morning until I take pity on them and let them in, whereupon they pad slowly across the floor and settle themselves in front of the fire for a day-long snooze.

So the cats certainly have their downsides. But they have many good qualities. The first is their talent for hunting. We've not seen a mouse or rat in the house since the day they arrived. They catch other things, too, of course. Many dead robins have been left on the front doormat. And decapitated frogs. They also torture and kill lizards. We once found a dead long-eared bat in a barn, and countless shrews have been eaten or killed and abandoned. Once I spotted Mandy beneath the car eating a wild bunny. When we drove off there was nothing left of the creature but a fluffy white tail.

But where the cats have really helped us has been with the children. Delilah in particular loves them very much. She takes Milly to bed and carries her around with her like a living doll. Delilah has a sentimental streak, and she says of herself: "I care for all animals. Not just nice ones. Even rats." She cried when I showed her a rat that I had killed with my air rifle. There is a lot of love between Delilah and the cats, and it's a joy to witness. It goes without saying that children enjoy looking after animals, feeding them, giving them water and stroking them. And the cats provide much amusement; the children particularly like to watch the cats play and hunt. Dusk seems to be the time when they come out to frolic, and they dash at amazing speeds across the yard and silently leap up trees with great agility and grace. The cats can also provoke great hilarity when playing with bits of string: I always think of the wonderful Fat Freddy's Cat cartoon strip in which the hippie owner Fat Freddy gleefully dances about, holding a piece of string for the cat to paw at. When the game is finished, the cat wanders off and reflects to itself: "Isn't it amazing how much fun one of them can have with a piece of string."

Finally, on the subject of cats, I would add that they are very beautiful creatures to have around the house. Our two are like moving cushions and arrange themselves in the most amazing shapes on sofas and chairs.

Now on to bunnies. Our first rabbit was christened Rosie Blossom Brownpatch ("because she has a brown patch," Delilah said). We loved her. She was a house bunny. She lived in the kitchen, and she was friendly and charming. It's true that she ate the curtains, but she was a clean bunny and provided a lot of fun and games. Even my mother loved her. And Delilah especially adored her. But then it all went wrong. Ask Delilah what happened and she will say: "Mummy killed her." Mummy did indeed drive over Rosie's back leg when the rabbit was playing in the yard. The vet said it would cost $1,500 to fix, so we decided to go for the cheaper option, which was to have the bunny put down. (Even that cost over $150.) Well, that was very sad. We'd loved that bunny. We all cried, except for Arthur, who coldly suggested that we get another one. So we did buy a new rabbit, and this one was called Lizzie Molly Flower Fast Bunny ("because she is a very fast bunny," Delilah said). She was sweet, but just not in the same league as Rosie Blossom. So when she decided she wanted to live outdoors, we let her go. Then began two glorious years. Our neighbor's white bunny, Felicity, was also living outside. The two rabbits became friends and lived somewhere in the barns. It was a wonderful sight, to drive down our lane and see one white and one black-and-white bunny dashing in all directions in that zigzag path that rabbits take. They were very canny: both managed to escape a vis-iting mixed-breed dog by dashing into secret little holes in the barns. Each evening both rabbits would come and mill about in the yard with all the other animals, so we would be treated to the delightful spectacle of the pony, the chickens, the rabbits and the cats all eating and playing together. Our farmer was amazed that the bunnies survived in the semi-wild as long as they did. But after two years of this fantastic menagerie, both rabbits vanished within a couple of days of each other. Whether they were taken by the fox—which had just dispatched all the chickens—or by the buzzard I had seen circling around, or whether they had gone deeper into the wild with the big jackrabbit we'd spotted once or twice hanging around in the yard, we'll never know. I hope they are living somewhere nearby in a cozy warren. But inside or out-side, a rabbit is a very good pet: comical, pretty, cute and a good size for little ones. "Of all animals rabbits are those that boys are most fond of," says Cobbett.

Those readers who would really like to embrace thrift might also consider breeding rabbits as a source of food. This was encouraged during the Second World War. Everyone knows that rabbits breed quickly and the meat is delicious: "Three does and a buck," says Cobbett, "will give you a rabbit to eat for every three days in the year." Each rabbit also provides a nice bit of fur. Why not sew them together and make a little coat for the child? Animals are very useful when properly processed. Eating them will also teach children that those bits of meat in the supermarket actually came from a real animal. And if you want to eat meat, should you not be prepared to take responsibility for the life and the death of the animal?

We have kept chickens and pigs for their eggs and pork, and in doing so we have saved a lot of money. But both are also real enhancements to daily life. The chicken is a curious and entertaining creature. They are actually very beautiful to look at. Think of chickens in art, particularly Gustav Klimt's *Garden Path with Chicken*. They possess an attractive mixture of dignity and innocence. They reward close study. They emit a wide range of clucking noises. They run in comically ungainly fashion, when pursued, for example, by Poppy, our black Labrador. Chasing the chickens has provided endless amusement for the children. Arthur also learned how to catch them (grab the tail feathers first). He waited until it was nearly dark and all the hens were roosting in their barn. He grabbed one quickly from behind and then made the amazing discovery that when you move a chicken's body around its head stays in the same place. Try it and you'll see.

Particularly magnificent is the gentlemanly cockerel. We decided to keep one on the advice of John Seymour, who writes: "Hens like having it off as much as we do." He also looks after the hens and of course there is the possibility of chicks. When you feed the flock, he makes noises to tell the hens that it's feeding time. He then stands back and waits till every hen has started to peck at the food, and only then will he move in for his portion. Every now and again he jumps on a hen, which teaches children about sexual reproduction: "Look, Daddy," Arthur said to me, without the hint of a snigger: "The cockerel is fertilizing the hen!"

Two years in a row our brood produced a few chicks, a miracle that happened by us simply following, again, John Seymour's advice and leaving them alone. No incubators or anything. The first year the chicks died, and we blamed the children. We did warn them that the chicks would not appreciate being given a bath. Both died and the children got a stern scolding. The following year, though, we watched three grow to near-maturity. One was a cockerel. Then the fox came visiting and every day took one or two chickens, until after a couple of weeks there was only the young cockerel left. He made it through a few days on his own, hanging out with the pigs for company, and then we returned home after a weekend away to find that he too had vanished. It was very, very sad to lose them all like that. I can still picture every one of them. You get to know them quite well.

But I suppose with all that drama happening around the animals, we have absolutely no need to get our drama second-hand from soap operas. The animals supply endless material for discussion.

As I have said, it is good for the kids to be picking up a few of the rudiments of husbandry, so they can better look after themselves in the future. Victoria has recently acquired a beehive, and she has taken Arthur to some of her beekeeping lessons. What a wonderful thing, to learn about bees, such an important element of civilization. Clearly also, after the collapse of our banking systems and the end of cheap oil, husbandry will be back in vogue, so it makes sense to accustom children to it now. Husbandry also demonstrates how work and play can be harmonized. For this chickens are very useful. It is enormously enjoyable to go and collect the eggs, and it is a job that can be easily delegated to a child. The feeding, also, can be done by a two-year-old. Arthur took charge of the egg production system, and he marketed the surplus by leaving a cash box at the end of the lane, some eggs in boxes, and a sign that read: "Free Range Egss [sic]. £1 for six." He also went door-to-door selling to the neighbors. Thus he educated himself in the principles of trade and made some of his own money, which was enormously satisfying to him. And when a child is in charge of some part of the household economy, such as the egg production, it means that he is actively and helpfully contributing to the household economy, which he loves to do. A burden and a hindrance no more. Children become a useful addition to the domestic labor force. And what is also important to the idle parent, they are learning that "getting a job" is not the only way to make money. As I have said elsewhere in this book, I will consider my education of my children to have been a success if they end up being self-employed in some way or other.

To learn about the source of our food is a useful part of every child's education, especially today when supermarkets and government rules have separated us so far from nature. Even if they dive into a world of convenience foods and supermarkets later in life, at least they will have grown up with a more complete picture of the relationships between animals and man and food. Having grown up with these sorts of ideas and skills will also make it that much easier for them to return to them later in life should they choose to.

We've not yet killed a chicken for eating, although we may do so soon. Right now we have no chickens, as a result of last year's fox attacks. But if it's anything like the other food we've produced at home, then we're in for a treat.

Hunting for food seems to me to be a terrific idea: rather than pay to shoot things in an amusement arcade, you go out and shoot them for free, and you come home with some food.

Then there is the pony. I have not always been in sympathy with it. It is expensive to keep. And it causes much extra toil and can damage things: last week it ate my vegetable patch. All the cabbages and broccoli plants that I had been lovingly tending for months vanished. That resulted in a lot of swearing. Amid the expletives I tried to argue to the pony's guardian, V, that this pony was entirely without practical use, that it was expensive and no one ever rode it anyway. "The kids like it," she said. "Not really! They only ride it about once a year!" I shouted back. The animal needs a lot of clearing up after as well. The yard is always full of horseshit, of which it produces a really unbelievable amount. Having said that, we have a limitless supply of good manure for the garden.

But as oil prices rise, ponies and horses begin to look like a good alternative to the motor car. You can buy small carts for $350, little three-seaters called "exercise carts." It strikes me that would be the perfect use for our old pony. We could take it for pub trips or shopping or picnics. And we could start a little business with it, giving pony rides to tourists. We could ferry holidaymakers from nearby Woody Bay Station to the beach and back. Perhaps Arthur could operate this venture and thereby contribute even more to the household income. We could paint a nice sign to go on the cart: "Arthur and Tom's Pony Rides" or some such. The business has a pleasing old-fashioned quality to it, a sensual real-life smell that is all too rare in these days of air-conditioning, Facebook, Bebo, and all the other anti-nature virtual worlds.

Cats, rabbits, chickens: I recommend all highly. We now also have a dog, and although I used to dislike dogs, this one is a jolly companion. My friend John recommends keeping a ferret in a hutch in the garden. Ferrets are supposed to be very useful for poaching. And one day I will take up Cobbett's advice and keep some pigeons in a dovecote: "They are very pretty creatures; very interesting in their manners; they are an object to delight children." I also hanker for a hawk. Again, hawks can hunt for you, thus providing for their keep. And we may at least inquire about barn owls, for they are beautiful and mysterious creatures.

If an animal is both useful and beautiful, then it is a welcome addition to the idle parent's household, because it saves money and gives the children a diversion, and also a feel for the care of animals. The noble pig fulfills all these criteria. We bought two young pigs in early June last year and fed them twice a day on scraps, nettles, and apples. It was very enjoyable to scratch them and watch their doings. Then we had them killed at home (although we have since found out that this is—absurdly—illegal, thanks to new legislation to encourage that all animals be killed in slaughterhouses) and spent two weeks processing them. The children now know exactly where their pork and bacon comes from. Although I have to admit that this morning, over his bacon, Henry started asking me some awkward questions:

"Is this our pig?" "Yes, Henry." "Why did we kill them?" "To eat them." "I didn't want to kill them." Oh dear. But our pigs did have the best life a pig could hope for, and the best death: a bullet to the head while eating. They didn't even have to suffer the stress of the journey to the slaughterhouse. A very great shame, then, that this ancient custom and right has now been outlawed by the state. I wrote about our pig-killing in a newspaper, and soon after received both a visit from the local health inspector and a rather ungrammatical letter from the Food Standards Agency's spookily titled "Director of Enforcement," saying: "Some of the practices you describe in your article are unlawful. . . . I am particularly concerned that people do not think they can kill animals in the way described in your piece."

Animals harmonize work and play, which is the ultimate aim of the idle family. Is it work or play to go and collect the eggs with Henry? To scratch the pigs' backs as they sit down and lean against the gate? To scatter chicken feed across the yard on a warm spring morning and watch as the hens scamper toward it with their strange sprinting waddle?

It is essential that children are able to indulge their wild natures. We should refute the urban ideal of an animal-free existence, a white plastic world of air-conditioned comfort, with no hens wandering past and shitting on the floor. That sort of vision is warned against in Huxley's *Brave New World*. It's a world where

animals are safely locked up in warehouses out of sight and processed quietly for food, having seen no soil or real light or animals
of other species, and having had no space to move around, whose
only companions are white-coated health and safety inspectors
with clipboards in their hands and hearts empty of love; where
animals are sliced by machine, packed into plastic wrap and taken
by giant trucks to the country's mega-markets, where we drive to
collect them.

With animals in the house, we keep the brave new world at
bay. Adults and children see the reality of nature in all its mess;
they see all the reality of life and death. Animals bring joy and
amusement into family life, they develop compassion in kids, and
they connect us all with nature.

15.

Make Stuff
from Wood and Junk

He must work like a peasant and think like a philosopher.

ROUSSEAU, *Émile*

Not long after we left the city, I found myself making things out of wood. I would go into the barn with a saw, a vice and a chisel and emerge with some objects that, in my view at least, closely resembled toys. There was the toy elephant that I somehow managed to carve. There was the rocket made from a log. With help from Arthur, I used the chisel to carve one end of the log into a point, and at the other end I nailed half a dozen pieces of red gas tubing for fire power. In the middle I carved an A, for "Arthur," and incredibly this piece is still in use today, three years after it was constructed. So, too, is the wooden airplane we made. Such toys are unique, and cost nothing, and we greatly enjoyed making them together. More recently we took apart an old Apple Mac computer and, having unscrewed the whole thing, were pleased to find that the plastic casing resembled a Darth Vader mask. Then we nailed bits of the computer to planks of wood to make a robot. Arthur nailed in two bits of red wire for its eyes. The end result was impressive: it looked like we'd crucified the computer. Arthur's wire eyes gave the effect of weeping blood: very effective. Our previous collaboration was called Wild Wood and consisted of three or four bits of wood nailed together and then covered with pieces of torn newspaper giving fragments of the news of the day. We are planning to make more such artworks and maybe even market them under the name Arthur and Tom, a sort of father-and-son version of Gilbert and George.

The children love puttering around in the workshop. And it's enjoyable and instructive for Dad too. Banging nails and sawing wood is deeply enjoyable, and being an idle parent is all about enjoyment and pleasure rather than self-sacrifice. We are always being told by child-care TV shows to set aside half an hour a day to "play" with them, but far better if our work and our play and our child care are all mixed up together into one happy and harmonious whole.

It's fascinating to read in Jean Liedloff's *The Continuum Concept* (the only book on children and babies worth reading; burn the rest, because they simply serve the status quo) that for her beloved Yequana Indians, work does not exist. They do not even have a word for it. Liedloff spent two and a half years with this South American tribe, observing their habits.

The boys, she writes, imitate their fathers. "Before they can talk, boys are provided with little bows and arrows that give valuable practice, as the arrows are straight and accurately reflect their skill." All parents notice this: children play at doing the things that their parents do. That is how they learn. Delilah and Arthur love helping me do the *Idler* subscription mail-out: bagging up and addressing five hundred copies of the magazine. So if you don't want your children to spend all their time at the computer, then don't spend all your time at the computer. Teach by example, not authority. If you don't have a workshop for making things, then convert the kitchen table into one. Be careful, too, of excessive praise and blame. Act like what they do is normal and expected when it's good. Too often we eject a torrent of praise so hyperbolic it sounds like surprise. As Liedloff remarks of Western families:

> If the child does something useful, like putting on his own clothes or feeding the dog, bringing in a handful of field flowers or making an ashtray from a lump of clay, nothing can be more discouraging than an expression of surprise that he has behaved socially. "Oh, what a good girl!" "Look what Georgie has made all by himself!" and similar exclamations imply that sociality is unexpected, uncharacteristic, and unusual in the child.

The idle parent, in contrast to the shrieking praising-and-blaming parent, should play it cool and expect the child to be cool as well. I'm not saying that I always manage this: instead of demonstrating the wisdom of cooperation, I shout "BE COOPERATIVE!" But I'm getting better, I hope. I also bear in mind the wisdom that one should keep one's trap shut a little more often. Some commentators are even of the opinion that you should not encourage your child in anything, and that this way the child will learn determination. Philip Pullman says that he was never encouraged to write by his parents. It was never made easy for him. But that itself gave him a forward thrust. Sometimes a mild discouragement from authority can be a real spur to creation.

Liedloff suggests that "children ought to accompany adults wherever they go." This, of course, is not easy with our modern working lives. *So change the situation.* Are full-time jobs for both parents and high-cost day care the only way we can imagine to organize our lives? It seems crazy to me. I used to love doing adult things with my parents when small (and also used to hate organized kids' activities, even birthday parties). I remember going into my parents' offices and finding them wondrous places. The highlight of Arthur's year when he was five was accompanying me to London where we spent two days clearing out the old office and loading up my van. He worked very well; he was a useful chap and good company. Far better for me than if I had been doing the work alone. There was no whining over those two days. Crucially, Arthur did not see the job as *work*. Like the Yequana, the idea of work as a "regrettable necessity," in Liedloff's words, did not exist for him. Our labor was simply a part of our life, and one to be enjoyed.

The Yequana, says Liedloff, laugh at discomfort. On one occasion she was helping them to move a large canoe through the forest. They kept dropping the thing and hurting their feet. Liedloff cursed the whole situation, but the Yequana, she writes, were in a particularly merry state of mind, revelling in the camaraderie. . . . Each forward move was for them a little victory. . . . I opted out of the civilized choice and enjoyed, quite genuinely, the rest of the portage. Even the barks and bruises I sustained were reduced with remarkable ease to nothing more significant than what they indeed were: small hurts which would soon heal and which required neither an unpleasant emotional reaction, such as anger, self-pity or resentment, nor anxiety at how many more there might be before the end of the haul.

And this was simply a question of mental attitude: the physical reality of the situation was unchanged. When we split the world into good things and bad things—work and leisure, right behavior and wrong behavior, intrinsically enjoyable activities and intrinsically unenjoyable activities—we sow the seeds of our own unhappiness and that of our children. Life will then become a never-fulfilled flight away from the "bad" and toward the "good." It may be best to say simply: "I like that" rather than "What a good boy." It's not too late! We can still help our children to enjoy their lives by starting to enjoy our own.

The dialectic of work=bad and life=good is one of Western society's most pernicious and controlling myths and must be smashed without delay. Incorporate your children into your life. Do what you want to do and let them follow. I have never found for a moment that having children stopped me doing what I wanted to do—bar going out to the odd dinner party, and who cares about that? All adults have seen children's innate creativity at work in the offerings they bring back from preschool and in their doings at home. Later, at school, that natural free-flowing urge to make things gives way gradually to supposedly more important tasks like passing exams.

Making things—things of beauty and use, and nearly everything homemade is beautiful—should be at the center of every child's experience. This activity should be thought of not as work but as play. Let them muck about. Do not confine. "Fear of the child's future leads adults to deprive children of their right to play," says A. S. Neill. John Locke shares the desire to make learning enjoyable for children:

> When he can talk, 'tis time he should begin to learn to read. But as to this, give me leave here to inculcate again . . . that a great care is to be taken that it never be made as a business to him, nor he look on it as a task. We naturally . . . even from our cradles, love liberty, and have therefore an aversion to many things, for no other reason, but because they are enjoined us.

Yes. Just this morning I was cursing Victoria for forcing me to help make the beds when I wanted to get on with writing this book. If I'd chosen to make the beds, though, I wouldn't have minded doing it. Locke continues: "I have always had a fancy that *learning* might be made a play and recreation to children."

Make work a "play" too. And making stuff from wood and old

junk is where work and play combine. By encouraging woodwork, we are also taking the first step to ensuring that as well as being good readers our children will have an introduction into the practical arts, what they used to call a "trade." Again, both Locke and Rousseau recommend working in wood as an essential part of their ideal education. Says Locke:

> I should propose . . . working in wood, as a carpenter, joiner or turner, these being fit and healthy recreations for a man of study or business. . . . The mind endures not to be constantly employed in the same thing or way; and sedentary or studious men should have some exercise, that at the same time might divert their minds and employ their bodies. . . . Besides, [he will] contrive and make a great many things both of delight and use.

Locke also recommends "husbandry in general" and points out that a varied life is a good life: "The great men among the ancients understood very well how to reconcile manual labor with affairs of state."

Rousseau, after unfairly castigating Locke for making an "effete" embroiderer of his young gentleman (I can find no such reference and conclude that Rousseau is just being mischievous), also praises woodwork:

> The trade I should choose for my pupil, among the trades he likes, is that of carpenter. It is clean and useful; it may be carried out at home; it gives enough exercise; it calls for skill and

industry, and while fashioning articles for everyday use, there
is scope for elegance and taste.

Yes, I would far rather my kids were doing something creative
and useful for exercise than something brutish and useless, like
a team sport. Team sports mercifully didn't seem to exist in
Locke's or Rousseau's time. Clearly they are a bastard child of in-
dustrialization. Much better, then, for parent and child to take
carpentry lessons together. Good for the idle parent, good for the
kids, fun and useful for everyone.

One problem here is that the anxious parent, conditioned
into living in fear by health and safety inspectors and worry-
inducing media, is afraid of hammers and nails and drills and
knives. But this is to underestimate children's built-in capacity for self-protection. When friends bring their kids around,
they look at our tree house with horror: I've even had to put up
a safety rail on the verandah—as if the kids are going to hurl themselves off the edge! They simply wouldn't. Our obsession with
safety removes independent judgment from the individual. It is
disabling. My friend Mark, on a trip down the Zaire, remembers
seeing small children playing on the deck of the huge boat with no
railings. "Aren't you worried they'll fall off?" he asked one
mother. "They're not stupid," came the laughing reply. Liedloff
says the same of the Yequana: from a young age they play with
knives and near the edge of deep pits. In primitive cultures the
good sense of the child is respected. We civilized parents actually
remove their confidence by shrieking "Careful!" at them the
whole time. Henry could scamper up and down the ladder, un-

supervised, to the tree house when he was two. But at three he had caught on to being frightened, and last week, for the first time ever, he called me to help him climb down. We must have taught him that fear—which is a terrible thought.

I would heartily recommend tree houses—the rougher the better. My friend Oli came to build ours, mostly out of junk. And the great thing is that it is unfinished. Arthur and Delilah are always adding new bits and painting it. Victoria has just suggested that we use pieces of an old child's bed to add to it (although her advice was to use them to make another safety rail!).

Another great advantage of working with wood is that it means avoiding the evil plastic, enemy of idleness. Wooden blocks are a particular joy: they last for ever and look good too. And if you get fed up with them, you can burn them. No landfill! How eco-friendly is that? In every way things made of wood are superior. Wood can be found for nothing. It can be mended and painted. It can be recycled, reused or burned in the fire. It grows on trees—no oil required. I understand that Steiner schools only have wooden toys, and that sounds to me like a thoroughly good idea.

In helping your kids to enjoy wood, *you* will enjoy wood again too. It reconnects us to the natural world, in a pleasurable revolt against the arid, clinical nature of plastic. My objection to the virtual computer worlds invented by California is that they separate us from the natural world, and indeed, that is part of the plan. One of the directors of the gigantic social networking site Facebook, Peter Thiel, has expressed a philosophy, based on Thomas Hobbes, which is essentially the idea that nature is hostile, a restrictive force to be overcome by man's boundless in-genuity. In cyberspace you can send virtual "gifts" though the ether, things that don't exist, that have none of the awkward real-ity of physical hand-made objects and can be enjoyed only through the medium of the screen. While this sort of thing can be enjoy-able in the short term, it simply is not real life and has none of the creativity and passion that making things out of wood offers. Making things out of wood makes us, each and every one, into an artist—not a "successful" artist who sells on the art market, but an artist nonetheless. The virtual world of the Californian futurist makes us into mere consumers of the visions of others.

Playing with wood connects us with the Robin Hood spirit, the greenwood, the Green Man, man and nature intertwined. Robin Hood and the outlaws lived in the forest and made their own dwellings (you can't get the planning permission to do this today). They allowed themselves to be absorbed by nature rather than building ramparts against it. That is why kids love to make dens in the woods: it is a primal instinct, handed down through gen-erations. And at the very least, a wood-filled childhood will give a child a confidence in practical matters which will serve him or her well from the point of view of everyday pleasure in life.

I will probably be scoffed at for arguing that a child's life and an adult's life should include a goodly portion of manual labor or craft. Surely, the scoffers will say, that sort of thing is now done in factories, generally in another country, leaving us free to waste time in virtual space? I think of a friend's story about a friend of his who had gone into business selling herbal highs and had made a lot of money. Previously he'd been a humble carpenter. Why the change? "Because," he said, "I got sick of rich people coming to my workshop and telling me how satisfying it must be to work with my hands."

Yet what is wrong with doing both? As Rousseau says, be a craftsman *and* a philosopher. Or an artist and a businessman. Rembrandt was a big-time property dealer, remember. You can read, write, make money in the morning and make things in the afternoon. Nothing so enjoyable as banging nails into wood. So let us fill our children's lives with variety, creativity and autonomy. And just as importantly, fill our own lives with variety, creativity and autonomy, and watch the lives of our children improve as a result. We are all artists.

16.

Say "Yes"

*One is inclined, in one's anarchic moments, to agree with
Louis Stevenson, that to be amiable and cheerful is a
good religion for a workaday world.*

JEROME K. JEROME, "On the Exceptional Merit Attaching
to the Things We Meant to Do," 1898

Oh, how we whine, we pampered parents of the West, attacked by choices, condemned to strive always to do the right thing, to get it right. We complain about money, we complain about lack of sleep, we complain about our partners, our co-workers, the buses, the newspapers, social networking sites, the government, telecom providers; we stamp our feet and shout at the usurers in the banking corporations and the swindlers and avaricious cheats in our cities; but most of all we complain about our own children. The first few months after the birth of the first baby are fairly blissful. Then the competing elements of the artificial constructions that we grandly call our "lives" become locked in mortal combat. We try to "get the balance right" between unenjoyable and enjoyable activities. We read newspaper columnists who whine, and we believe, wrongly, that because they whine, our own whining is justified (we forget that their whining is a profitable business—they make money from moaning, whereas our suffering is strictly nonprofit). But we are moaning about the very lives that *we* have created for ourselves. We took that job, we bought that flat, we chose that boyfriend or girlfriend, we had that baby, we bought that car, we chose that broadband provider, we gave our money to that bank, we live in this city, and we live in this country. We were free to go and retire alone in Goa and live on the beach for the rest of our lives, childless and free. But we chose not to do that. And then we complained!

But are we hungry? Are we cold? Are we homeless? Are we in jail? No. Are we free to change our lives, to quit our jobs, walk out on our homes, leave our wives or husbands? Yes. The point is, if you are not happy with your situation, then you should change it. And do not believe that you are powerless, because you yourself created the situation that you now find yourself in. You also created the mental attitude that you have toward that situation, and similarly, if you so chose, you could re-create that mental attitude. This is not to say that pain is not real. Bereavements, domestic conflict, financial disasters . . . as Blake, the bard of Albion, wrote:

Man was made for joy and woe;
And when this we rightly know,

Through the world we safely go.

Joy and woe are woven fine,

A clothing for the soul divine.

What we so often observe in the old-fashioned cultures is a stoical attitude to life, an inspiring lack of self-pity, and these attitudes are still to be found in societies that to us look extremely limited in terms of the life choices available. What you get in rich societies, by contrast, is a hell of a lot of moaning. And it seems that the richer people are, the more moaning there is to be done. Rich people always complain about poor service in hotels. They complain about lazy staff or staff who are always ill. They complain about airlines, call-center workers, taxi companies. Indeed, riches seem to create more causes for complaint, possibly because riches multiply the number of transactions in a person's life, thereby increasing the possibility of things going wrong. Whereas when you keep things simple, less goes awry. Riches also create an arrogant lack of patience: I can pay, so why should I have to wait?

My friend John Lloyd, the producer of such British television shows as *Blackadder* and *Spitting Image* and more recently the originator of the *QI* series, has observed a phenomenon at middle-class dinner parties that he calls "moasting," an unpleasant combination of moaning and boasting. Complaining about the chalet girl in Gstaad, or about poor treatment at the hands of Virgin Upper Class, or how the Eton English master is not up to scratch. To bring two unpleasant phenomena into one intensely awful new form of whining takes a particularly British form of negative genius.

Both should be avoided at all costs by the idle parent. (As with all these suggestions, bear in mind that the idle parent is against fanaticism in every form. A bit of whining in moderation will not have the Idle Police knocking.) Whining is the adult's mirror image of the child's whining. When they hear us whining about things, children assume it's normal to complain, and therefore they whine (powerlessness is the other cause, as we have seen). Indeed, we encourage them to whine and complain, by continually probing them for their judgment on things: Did you have a good time? Was it fun? Is it a good book? What did you think of the film? How was school? It's what the ancient Chinese called the "discriminating mind," the false setting up of good things and bad things. This discriminating mind is really a way of making children into consumers, because consumers are the biggest whiners of all, always ready to fire off complaints to customer service representatives, whatever they may be, and always ready to buy better products. Living your life through your selection of products and services is the whining principle put into action. The non-consumer, the creator, knows that all things are equal. He is enlightened, he has the "non-discriminating mind" and has nothing to complain about. He has a cheerful Stoic disposition and would tend to agree with Epicurus's epigram:

Wealth consists not in having great possessions, but in having few wants.

Having many wants clearly creates whining. Having a vague, abstract idea of how things could be rather than celebrating how they are creates a sense of discontent. Let us rejoice in our own uniqueness, our own difference, our own eccentricity.

John Stuart Mill, himself the product of a hothouse education planned out by his father, James Mill, with the evil Panopticon inventor Jeremy Bentham, was in sympathy with the idea of the simple life, and indeed, he attributed its ongoing discussion in the mid–nineteenth century to the work of Rousseau. In *On Liberty*, he writes: "The superior worth of simplicity of life, the enervating and demoralizing effect of the trammels and hypocrisies of artificial society, are ideas which have never been entirely absent from the cultivated mind since Rousseau wrote."

We must take personal responsibility. That way lies freedom from whining. Take Mill's wise words on education, which most of us leave to an external agency:

> If the government would make up its mind to require for every child a good education, it might save itself the trouble of providing one. It might leave to parents to obtain the education where and how they pleased, and content itself with helping to pay the school fees of the poorer classes of children, and defraying the entire school expenses of those who have no one else to pay for them. The objections which are urged with reason against State education do not apply to the enforcement of education by the State, but to the State's taking upon itself to direct that education: which is a totally different thing. . . . A general State education is a mere contrivance for moulding people to be exactly like one another . . . it establishes a despotism over the mind, leading by natural tendency to one over the body.

Why does the state have to exert so much control over state education? Why can't they leave teachers alone? Mill is right that few parents would complain if they were given education vouchers that could be redeemed at any school. It is the ideological control that we object to.

So we whine about our schools, whether they be private or state. Moaning about the private school we have chosen for our child is an example of "moasting" at its most absurd, but moaning about any school is ridiculous, since there are plenty of alternatives available, including homeschooling and learning groups. Once you've made your bed you should lie in it, and if you don't like it, get out.

It's the same with children. We are not obliged to have children. We choose to have them. There are many other paths through life. By not whining about it, we are surely setting a good example to our children, who will learn by example that if we are unsatisfied with a situation, then it is entirely within our power to adjust either the situation itself or our attitude to that situation.

Now, instead of whining and moaning and wishing that things would somehow change, take my advice and learn to say "Yes!" to your kids. This very simple idea was suggested to me by John Lloyd. He said that he had noticed in his own life how much he was *fobbing off* his kids: from the early days, when he would linger late at the office because that seemed preferable to facing the mewling infant and general chaos of home, to later, when the kids were a little older, when he would become angry if disturbed by a child in the middle of a phone call. I have noticed this tendency in myself: sometimes I am staring at my computer screen and a child comes into my study and asks to play a game: "Will you play Tractor Ted with me?" Self-importantly, I sigh and say something along the lines of "I'm working" or, worse, a querulous "Can't you see I'm working?" The child persists for a while and then gives up. I then look at my screen again and wonder whether checking the Amazon ranking of my last book can really be considered to be important work. Can it not be left for five minutes? Lloyd pondered these questions and decided to start saying "yes" to his children when he was on the phone or working and they asked him for something. He realized, too, that their repeated requests and irritating behavior toward him were a sort of demand for recompense for earlier love starvation. So he would put the phone down and go and play with the child.

Isn't this rather a lot of work for the idle parent? Not really. The child will be delighted with his five minutes of mucking about. And in any case, it's actually a pleasure for the parent. After all, you'll have plenty of time to work and stare at the screen as they grow older and less interested in you. Enjoy them while you can!

John also points out that saying "yes" can be seen as a sort of investment for the idle parent. After you have made a habit of saying "yes" for a while, say a year or two, the kids will stop bothering you in the same way. Your yay-saying will have installed security in their hearts, so that they will no longer have the need to test your love and continually press for it.

Let us call this method the Lloyd Plan for Happy, Stress-Free Parenting. Here it is:

Despite the way it looks to those of us who are already parents—and making the customary hash of it—parenting is actually a glorious opportunity for a lifetime of idleness. There's a really simple knack to this. Give children whatever they want, whenever they want it, as soon as they ask. If children know they can have your undivided attention for any reason, no matter how paltry, at any time of day or night, lo and behold, miracle of miracles, they stop asking. This leaves you free to fart around doing whatever it was you formerly considered more important.

The Lloyd Plan has something in common with the ideas in *The Continuum Concept*. If you give the kid unlimited "in arms" time, as Liedloff calls it, when small, he will leave you alone later:

The need for physical contact tapers off quickly when [the child's] experience quota has been filled, and a baby, tot, child or adult will require the reinforcement it gives him only in moments of stress with which his current powers cannot cope. These moments become increasingly rare, and self-reliance grows with a speed, depth and breadth that would seem prodigious to anyone who has known only civilized children deprived of the complete in-arms experience.

The person in charge of the baby—whether that is the mother or father or a relation—does not hover and "do things" with the child, but is always at hand:

Among the Yequana the attitude of the mother or caretaker of a baby is relaxed, attentive to some other occupation than baby-minding but receptive at all times to a visit from the crawling or creeping adventurer. She does not stop her cooking or other work unless her full attention is actually required. She does not throw her arms open to the little seeker for reassurance but, in her calm way, allows him the freedom of her person, or an arm-supported ride on her hip if she is moving about.

Liedloff goes on to praise the very passivity of the parent:

She does not initiate the contacts nor contribute to them except in a passive way. It is the baby who seeks her out and shows her by his behavior what he wants. He is the active, she the passive agent in all their dealings; he comes to her to sleep when he is tired, to be fed when hungry. His explorations of the wide world are counterpointed and reinforced by his resort to her and by his sense of her constancy while he is away.

The idle parent needs to harmonize the two at-first-sight different attitudes of doing nothing and saying "yes." Let them come to you, but when they do come to you, be there for them and try not to fob them off. This way you will have plenty of time to pursue your own business, whatever that may be, and the child will learn self-reliance and the feeling of being loved from the beginning. Being loved but being free. Do less! Passive parenting is responsible parenting.

Being hassled by your kids—I love my friend Heather's comment to her imploring child, "Will you stop terrorizing me?"—is a direct result of you having starved them of being-there time in the past. We are all told by our non-contemplative society to be active parents, so we rush around, work, and then jump into our kids' faces when we do see them and get, like, really active. It is surely wiser for parents to arrange things so they are both at home as much as possible during the first one to three years of the child's life, and to organize things so that there is a constant presence in that time of helpers in the form of relatives, friends, neighbors or nanny if funds allow. The more people around, the merrier. It lightens the burden for the lone mom, who was never, ever meant to do all this on her own. Crazy idea! Better to have lots of time than lots of money in those early years. There will be time later for earning.

Stopping the whining and saying "yes" to your kids could help you to accept your life as it is in other areas. One simple trick is to turn off the radio. Here is Aldous Huxley writing in 1946:

> Listening four or five times a day to newscasters and commentators, reading the morning papers and all the weeklies and monthlies—nowadays, this is described as "taking an intelligent interest in politics." St John of the Cross would have called it indulgence in idle curiosity and the cultivation of disquietude for disquietude's sake.

Dissatisfaction breeds moaning, therefore we need to remove the causes of dissatisfaction. One cause of dissatisfaction is a tendency to feel a failure, that things are not perfect, the way they are portrayed by images in magazines and on screens. So we need to abandon the quest for perfection and give ourselves up to Providence. Huxley again:

> The popular philosophy of life has ceased to be based on the classics of devotion and the rules of aristocratic good breeding, and is now moulded by the writers of advertising copy, whose one idea is to persuade everybody to be as extroverted and uninhibitedly greedy as possible, since of course it is only the possessive, the restless, the distracted, who spend money on the things that advertisers want to sell.

Perhaps we need a little more quietude, a little more rest, a little more kindness, a little more cheerfulness and a lot less greed.

17

Learn How to Live from Your Kids

A man shall become truly poor and as free from his own
creaturely will as he was when he was born.

MEISTER ECKHART

dle parents will never sacrifice themselves to their children. They will carry on with their own lives, and the kids will learn and grow in the slipstream. But they will respect their little creatures and observe their ways with interest. Children say funny things. And you can always learn from them. The important thing in parenting is not what you *do* but your relationship with your child. It is how you *are* that counts. Rather than try to follow a list of somebody else's rules, we must concentrate first and foremost on our mental attitude toward our children. And a certain sense of gratitude toward them for being in our lives may be one way to start.

When your first baby is born you learn the meaning of uncon-
ditional love. It's a new kind of love, different from the love you
may or may not feel toward your parents and different from the
carnally charged love that you feel (or felt) toward your partner.
Every human heart is touched by the presence of a baby because
the baby has not yet been conditioned and commodified. God
knows, the businessmen try! When our eldest child was born, we
were presented, minutes after the birth, with a gift pack containing a name-brand diaper, a pack of wet wipes and some cou-
pons for some awful baby-industry product. From the cradle to
the branded grave, we are ever exploited as money spenders and
consumers.

But the baby is as yet unaware of this. He has only his animal-
like body and big staring eyes. Is it wonder or is it just a sort of
oneness that we see in the child? An undivided self, perhaps. My
friend Penny Rimbaud is of the opinion that small children are
neither naturally good nor naturally bad—but are rather simply
passionate. They are full of passion for living. Their crying and
their laughing are both expressions of the same fundamental lust
for life. Well, I hope this is true because at this very moment, as I
write, I can hear Henry pumping out the most horrifying screams.
He sounds like he is being tortured. Maybe he is being tortured.
Any moment now Victoria will call out for my help. Oh, woe!

What is the fate of the baby coming into the world? Not a
happy one, according to Blake in "Infant Sorrow":

> My mother groan'd, my father wept:
> Into the dangerous world I leapt,

Helpless, naked, piping loud,
Like a fiend hid in a cloud.
Struggling in my father's hands,

Striving against my swaddling bands,
Bound and weary, I thought best
To sulk upon my mother's breast.

(A note on swaddling: It was a common medieval practice, but Rousseau thought it cruel and unnatural, and so, clearly, did Blake. Swaddling has made a comeback recently, promoted by books on strict baby routines. But the idle parent surely wants to let the kid wave its arms around freely?)

It's a dangerous world indeed for the poor infant to be thrust into. He resists it, he rebels against its strictness and regimentation and isolation. He screams for people to come and hold him. But they ignore him. There is something wrong here, he seems to be saying. And then mothers are told that he's just crying out for attention, and best to leave him to cry. This seems a little cruel. Anyway, the small baby has not yet been tamed and forced to accept capitalist clock time and the man-created work ethic. All is one to him. He is in the moment. Some of our most unpleasant scenes as a family have happened during the morning rush for school. The school bus leaves from the end of the lane at 8:30 a.m., and the children have to be dressed, washed, bagged up and ready. How they resist being told what to do and torn away from doing something they were enjoying! "Put your shoes on!" *"Put your shoes on!"* "PUT YOUR SHOES ON!" Why do they resist authority? Because they are living in the moment, in the here and now. And maybe—just maybe—when kids dawdle, it is not they who are at fault but the system that attempts to regiment them so strictly. When the kids rebel against it, perhaps they are really the sane ones. They still have some dignity: like the young Thomas De Quincey, who was described by his parents as the "imperious young sultan" of the family.

That is why we should listen to our children more. They have much to teach us about the natural ways of life. Such as:

(a) Living in the Present

As adults we perpetually make efforts to remove our children from the present and thrust them into the future or the past. We ask questions that emphasize past experience: "How was school? What did you do today? Which was the best part?" "Did you enjoy that film? Was it fun?" We also plan for the future and teach them how to look forward to things (perhaps in order to make the terrible present more bearable): "Are you excited about Christmas?" "Are you looking forward to our trip to Chuck E. Cheese's?" From an early age, it seems that we attempt to teach children that the "now" is not a good place—but rather that life was lived in the past or will be lived in the future. Children's resistance to answering questions such as "How was school?" (always a conversation non-starter) is perhaps a sign that really they want simply to *be*, to continue doing what they are immersed in, right now. This would also explain their resistance to punctuality and unwillingness to be called away from something they are enjoying in order to come and eat their supper. (I'm planning to buy a dinner gong, so I don't have to keep shouting for them. I also have a fantasy where they play outside all day and I go outside and ring a big bell at six o'clock to summon them in from the fields. . . .)

Every parent knows well the frustrations of going for a walk with a toddler. They simply do not seem to understand the idea of destination, of getting from A to B. Instead, they insist on daw-dling and puttering, bending down to pick things up, looking at signs, even—maddeningly—going backward. Enjoying them-selves, I suppose, is what it is. Very frustrating to the goal-centered adult. "Come on, Henry," we bleat with false jollity, in case we are being observed, with that little indulgent half-smile on our lips. But walking with toddlers, if viewed from a different perspective, can be enjoyed. The toddler may teach the adult to engage with the pleasure of the here and now, without a care for what has been or what is to come. The toddler can plant the adult firmly in the mo-ment. Yea, cease striving, and give in to what is happening! And the more you allow them simply to be in the moment, the more chance they have of teaching you in turn how to live in the mo-ment, and therefore how to free yourself of anxiety, regret and fear. Small children are providential creatures: they think of their passionate lives right now, and the future and the past are mean-ingless abstract concepts. The future is not real. It does not exist (in fact, as I have often argued, the future is a capitalist concept, because our fears about it can be manipulated to make us spend money on insurance plans, pensions, property and so on).

(b) Being Silly and Laughing in the Face of Disaster

"You're a poo-poo head, Daddy," the little ones say to me, and titter. The substitution of words with the word "poo," and indeed the word's liberal use in any sentence, is, as has been observed by the semiologist Gregory Rowland, a cornerstone of the wit of small children. But they're right, it's funny. Children love to play with words, they love jokes, and most jokes are based around puns or wordplay. And they love pulling faces and tumbling and making farty noises. And so do I. Face-pulling is a good one: it was a medieval game. Make everyone in the room pull a horrible face. Take pictures, if you like. Then judge the winner. It's an idea I might take to our village fête next year. Maybe with a Polaroid camera. Anyway, it's great fun. And it's wonderful to have kids as an excuse to be able to express all that silliness again. Human beings are naturally fun-loving, but we lose this instinct as we grow older, serious and businesslike. Kids remind us of the things that really matter.

Children also seem to possess an innate delight in the rupturing of everyday order. Put the wrong word in a sentence and they will guffaw helplessly. They also love it when things go wrong in the adult world, when, as Penny Rimbaud would put it, "consensual reality breaks down." That is the reason for their fascination with fire engines—somewhere the ordered universe of the grown-ups has gone kaput. In the same way that some people love a road accident and will crowd around the scene of the crash offering advice, so kids love it when the clock-bound parental systems grind to a halt. That, after all, is when the natural humanity and generosity of people emerge. Disasters can be a sort of liberation from the grim efficiency of industrial capitalism. When my brother and I were growing up, one of our favorite stories was about the time we had to be rescued from the rocky coast of North Devon by a helicopter, because my dad had got the tide times wrong. And indeed I can remember that incident almost perfectly, even today, such was the intense pleasure of that rapture. Another time we were on a skiing holiday and my brother and I went each morning on our own to buy a Fanta. One morning my brother dropped his glass on the floor, smashing it into tiny pieces. We looked up at the café owner, expecting to be told off. But instead he gave a huge bellowing laugh, a wonderful and entirely correct response to mess. I am always getting angry with Henry for spilling things. But wouldn't it be better to laugh at the mess? Getting angry doesn't help to clear it up.

They say that children like routine, but do they? The times that stand out for me from my childhood are the times when the routine was broken: fire alarms at school, broken glasses, the stray match that landed in the fireworks box, cars breaking down. Broken routine adds intensity to life. I am slowly learning from my own children to enjoy disasters when they happen. On Christmas Eve last year my van broke down on a roundabout when we were on our way to visit relatives. I was on my own with three kids in the back and no cell phone. I suffered a moment of irritation, but what followed was in fact quite enjoyable. We walked over the roundabout to the gas station, where the staff let me use their phone to call the towing service. The children had a McDonald's milk shake and fries, a rare treat in this anticonsum-erist family. Back at the van, by pure chance, someone I knew from home, a hundred miles away, saw us and pulled over to help. He towed us off the roundabout and out of danger. Then the tow-truck driver arrived. And the police. And then Victoria, who was traveling in the other car. It was quite a party down there on the Hazelgrove roundabout on the A303. I met lots of people and had a good time. And I came away with a good story to tell. When I mentioned that I'd broken down to adults at parties, they put on a sympathetic face, automatically assuming that it was a "night-mare" (that overused word), but I'd put them right and explain what enormous fun the whole thing had been. Somehow, in the middle of disaster you give yourself up to Providence and delight in the failure of man's plans. And it was the children who taught me how to enjoy it. I distinctly remember making the deliberate choice to view the incident as an adventure rather than an insup-portable inconvenience. I looked at the situation from their point of view and saw a story, a tale, an expedition. The secret is to not take life too seriously but to laugh at it all the time, as children do. That way lies the strength to cope with hardships.

(c) Drawing and Playing Tricks and Games

Delilah sits and sketches for hours. One day she said she wanted to stop watching the video they had on—it was *Babe*—and go to bed to draw. Her cats are particularly delightful. Henry's scribbles are improving. He asks for a pad of paper in the evening so he can scribble in bed like Delilah. Arthur wants to draw birds. Magic is another of Arthur's interests, and I recommend to any parent to learn some tricks. Now Arthur and I can perform a trick together in which the spectator chooses a card from the pack, then Arthur hurls the pack at the window, whereupon all the cards fall to the floor except the one chosen, which is stuck to the glass—on the other side of the window! We also play chess and checkers and backgammon. And why, oh why, do people not play cards more often? A pack of cards costs just a dollar or two, but it offers infinitely more fun and variety than a Sony PlayStation, is more portable, can involve any number of players and can be meditated upon in quiet moments. And, of course, it is self-sufficient, requiring no power source. A simple idle-parenting tip would be to play cards every evening after supper, at least in the winter months.

(d) Discovering That Work and Play Can Be the Same Thing

Henry loves nothing more than loading up logs into his tractor and unloading them at the other end of the yard. In this way he taught me to regard what I had previously regarded as an irksome task as a pleasurable pastime. Isn't it crazy that a forty-year-old man, with all his years of experience and all his self-satisfaction, cannot use his mind to enjoy working, as a child does? We have already seen how Locke and Rousseau developed this idea when planning their ideal education. The same idea is in Plato. It emerges also in Cobbett's *Rural Rides* from 1830, when Cobbett describes how his son Richard taught himself to read and then how he got his son to begin to learn arithmetic: "He had learned from mere play, to read, being first set to work of his own accord, to find out what was said about Thurtell [a notorious murderer who was hanged in 1824], when all the world was talking and reading about Thurtell." Cobbett set Richard some sums, but first he explained that there was a practical purpose behind arithmetic, which was to keep business accounts. Then he simply left sums lying around, and Cobbett said that Richard learned much very quickly, because he had chosen to learn:

> Now when there is so much talk about education, let me ask how many pounds it generally costs parents to have a boy taught this much of arithmetic; how much time it costs also; and, which is a far more serious consideration, how much mortification and very often how much loss of health, it costs the poor scolded broken-hearted child, who becomes dunder-headed and dull for all his lifetime, merely because that has been imposed on him as a task which he ought to regard as an object of pleasurable pursuit.

Children, then, teach us that work and play can be the same thing, and we in turn can use that insight to help them to learn useful things. If work is voluntary, autonomous, creative—freely undertaken—then can it really be called work? It is the urgent task of the idle parent to collapse this distinction in his or her own life and in the lives of his or her children, if the parent craves self-reliance and happiness.

(e) Learning the Pleasures of Dens

According to Friedensreich Hundertwasser, the great twentieth-century artist and architect, eco-housing pioneer and abhorrer of straight lines, all people should build their own houses. To him, the most beautiful homes were self-built huts he saw in northern Africa and, indeed, children's dens. He divided each human being into a spiritual trinity:

1. The person in the building
2. The architect
3. The builder

In the ideal world, Hundertwasser said, 1, 2 and 3 will be the same person. And this is precisely what occurs with the self-built dens of children. Children instinctively want to design and build their own homes, away from the realm of professionals and parents. When they build their dens, children take control of the means of production: they are the inhabitants, the architects and the builders. So the den helps to unite in harmony three aspects of life that modern civilization so often splits up, professionalizes and outsources. This accounts for the deep and intense pleasure that den building brings to children. Even just an old door leaned against a wall is a statement of the will to independence and creativity. Den building also accords with the spiritual principle of using what you already have under your nose: den makers do not drive to the hardware superstore and buy the materials. Today our natural den-building instinct has been commodified and exploited by the IKEAs and the Habitats, the salesmen of flat-pack furniture and paint. Whereas to decorate our own den is a perennial pleasure.

So learn from the kids and make dens, build sheds, tree houses, benders in the woods, Eeyore houses. My next plan, having sold my van, is to buy a dinky caravan and make that pretty inside. Caravans and camper vans are a version of dens for adults, this time on wheels. Think also of the child's fascination with birds' nests and animals' underground houses, those self-built dwelling places. We should all build our own houses: it is not a childish thing to do; it is a natural thing to do, and the child is merely expressing a natural need that modern civilization takes away.

(f) The Pleasure of Making Noise

Children make a real racket. We are always complaining about the noise they make. But we should learn that noisemaking is, again, a natural urge that often goes unexpressed in adult life. I think we should indulge ourselves in the odd bit of pot banging and shouting, preferably around a fire. You don't need to be musically gifted to hit a saucepan with a wooden spoon or sing a simple song. But it helps to get someone in who knows what he's doing. To this end, I recently invited the conductor Charles Hazlewood to orchestrate a Christmas music event in our local village hall. He based the evening around the old tradition of wassailing, where groups of people go from door to door, singing and demanding to be given food and hot punch. What they sing is called a wassail, and what they get is also called a wassail:

> Wassail and wassail all over the town,
> The cup it is white, and the ale it is brown,
> The cup it is white like the old ashen tree,
> And so is the malt of the best barley.

A famous example of a wassail is "We Wish You a Merry Christmas," which of course contains the lines:

> Oh, bring us some figgy pudding;
> Oh, bring us some figgy pudding;
> Oh, bring us some figgy pudding,
> And a cup of good cheer.

And later the lines:

> We won't go till we get some;
> We won't go till we get some;

We won't go till we get some,

So bring some out here.

Under Charlie's tutelage, we learned to sing these songs while banging pots and pans to keep ourselves in time. All the kids loved the singing and the noisemaking. And so did the adults, although of course the adults were much more stiff and awkward about the whole thing.

Another example of noisemaking in ritual form is the old custom of Rough Music, a pre-industrial tradition that is described by the great historian E. P. Thompson. Rough Music was a sort of ritual expression of hostility against a local character, perhaps a wife beater. It consisted, writes Thompson, of

raucous, ear-shattering noise, unpitying laughter, and the mimicking of obscenities. It was supported, in Thomas Hardy's description, by "the din of cleavers, tongs, tambourines, kits, crouds, humstrums, serpents, ram's horns, and other historical kinds of music." But if such "historical" instruments were not to hand, the rolling of stones in a tin kettle—or any improvization of draw-tins and shovels—would do. In a Lincolnshire dialect glossary (1877) the definition runs: "Clashing of pots and pans. Sometimes played when any very unpopular person is leaving the village or being sent to prison."

The purpose of such ritualized noisemaking was partly to avoid real violence. Rough Music can be seen as a release of pressure, an outlet for some innate human need. I recommend a bit of Rough Music at home. Just get the saucepans, put a stone in a baked-beans tin, hand out the instruments and make a procession around the house. Make up a song or a wassail. When you grow in confidence, you could perhaps take your rough wassail out on to the streets and do it there. The point is that, just as children need to make some noise, so do we adults, and we would do well, again, to learn from the kids.

(g) Loving Liberty

As John Locke wisely observed, children are lovers of liberty. They resist confinement. They appear to have naturally imperious, even insolent natures. Clearly the purpose of "civilizing" through parental nagging and school-based education systems is to squash the imperiousness and introduce docility. To make slaves out of gods. That the kids resist the process tooth and nail should be celebrated. Might their resistance not demonstrate that there is something at fault with the enclosing system rather than the things enclosed? We should learn from these liberty-lovers to resist enclosure ourselves, rather than attempting to drag the kids down to our slavish level. Forget ideas of "good" and "bad" behavior. Keep instead the poles of "free" and "enslaved" in your mind. Reduce authority and enlarge freedom. Revere and respect the little creatures in your house. As Bertrand Russell wrote in "Freedom Versus Authority in Education": "Reverence for human personality is the beginning of wisdom, in every social question, but above all in education."

And the first step should be to revere your own human personality and treat yourself well. More noise, more freedom, more silliness, less importance, right here, right now!

18.

Good Books
and Bad Books

*To most kinds of men it is an extraordinary delight to study. For
what a world of books offers itself, in all subjects, arts, and
sciences, to the sweet content and capacity of the reader.*

ROBERT BURTON, *The Anatomy of Melancholy*

Researchers are always telling us that a houseful of books will
set up a child with a lifelong interest in learning. Books are
useful. They are friends and companions. Technologically
they have never been surpassed. They are perfect: portable, made
from renewable materials, able to display both words and pictures, and with no need for batteries.

But we have to be careful. There are a lot of very bad books out
there, which though they cost just $3.99 contain only about
seventeen words and are deadly boring to the adult. For example,
Disney movie spin-off books that attempt to retell an entire

movie in a few pages are generally poorly written and usually not worth much of anyone's time.

So rather than submit to popular opinion on these matters and allow any old book to litter the house, just because it is a "book" and books are seen as good, you should only allow good books, and by good I do not mean "containing edifying moral instruction" but good in the sense of being well written and offering an entertaining story. We need to be on our guard against the moralists and remember that the early Puritans championed the spread of literacy because it made their job of brainwashing easier.

We should also bear in mind that Rousseau was against books: "I hate books," he writes in *Émile*, a phrase intended to provoke rather than to be taken as literally true. Why? Because he was attempting to provide a natural childhood, naturalness and a rejection of the modern world being necessary adjuncts to liberation: "Civilized man is born and dies a slave. The infant is bound up in swaddling clothes, the corpse is nailed down in his coffin. All his life long man is imprisoned by our institutions. . . . Society has enfeebled man."

Nowadays, this sentiment seems truer than ever. And it is made even worse by the fact that we are not only "imprisoned by our institutions" but also trapped by commerce into existing merely as consumers. Books, says Rousseau, are not natural:

> Without the study of books, such a memory as the child may possess is not left idle; everything he sees and hears makes an impression on him, he keeps a record of men's sayings and

doings, and his whole environment is the book from which he unconsciously enriches his memory. . . . I hate books; they only teach us to talk about things we know nothing about.

Plato had a similar attitude to books: he thought that they made people lazy. They would not bother to learn or remember something if it was written in a book. An overreliance on books— our equivalent today would be an overreliance on the computer screen, Google and the mouse—might well tend to retard the development of the memory. It's hard, though, to imagine us returning to the bookless life of the noble savage, noble though the savage might be. And I personally derive a great deal of pleasure from reading aloud to my children, and in reading myself, and in seeing them read. But when I read to my kids, I need genuinely to enjoy the book myself. This is the key: to find books that both parties will enjoy. And that really is the aim of this chapter: I want to suggest a few good books, not morally instructive books but rollicking good reads that will be with you for ever.

I'm going to recommend some poetry, too, because poetry is often forgotten, and reading good poetry to your kids is a way of reigniting your own pleasure in it. And think how much good poetry there is out there to be discovered—thousands of years' worth. It's vitally important that the parent enjoys the reading. If you don't enjoy the book, then you tend to rush through it, surreptitiously flicking ahead to see how many more pages are left. Not that we should feel too guilty about this: with kids of pre-reading age, why not skip words, phrases or even whole pages? They'll never know, and you'll reach the end, kiss them good night, turn off the light and bound down the stairs to the kitchen for that first bottle of beer all the quicker.

But find good-quality material and everyone is happy. There is really no reason for the parent to be bored. Particularly to be avoided are those books that try to behave like a toy at the same time. For example, we have a book with wheels on the bottom, so it's supposed to be a toy tractor and a book about tractors at the same time, but it ends up being a bad toy and a bad book. And have you noticed that many books glorify machines and amplify the myth of progress? Henry has one such book that keeps insisting that in the old days everyone had to work very hard, but that today the combine harvester, for instance, can do the work of twenty men and isn't it wonderful. Pure propaganda. The book doesn't offer the alternative view, that men used to enjoy working in teams and that the combine harvester has helped destroy farm life by making the work lonely, geared only around making a profit rather than combining work with a pleasurable everyday life.

Worse still are those book/jigsaw puzzles. All the pieces are immediately lost because there is no box to keep them in. Who comes up with these daft ideas? Ambitious young men in the big toy companies' product development departments, I suppose. And why do we buy them? We should never, ever, buy costly nothings like LeapPads and all the rest. You do not need a machine to learn how to read. And those gadgets date in seconds, whereas real books last lifetimes. Save the money for more beer or wine or real books.

So, here is my list. With little expense, you can assemble a superb library. Most of the following I bought secondhand or found in thrift shops; some were mine when I was small, and some seem just to have appeared.

1. Allan and Janet Ahlberg (b. 1938; 1944–1994)

I don't much like modern kids' books. Most are dull and work only to promote the dominant values of society to children, that hard work and machinery are good. But I make an exception for the brilliant Ahlbergs and, in particular, *Each Peach Pear Plum* and also *Peepo!*—the only novelty book (each board page has a hole through which you can spy a detail from the following page) that I recommend. The pictures are funny, and I get a kick out of the lovingly drawn period interiors.

2. J. M. Barrie (1860–1937), *Peter Pan*

Peter Pan, of course, is an Edwardian classic by Scottish author J. M. Barrie, who also wrote *My Lady Nicotine*, a delightful work in praise of smoking, and was a contemporary of Jerome K. Jerome. His *Peter Pan* is a classic study of the desire for freedom and, in common with the best children's books, features a land free of parental intrusion: there are no authority figures. The book was written in 1904 and Barrie's intention was to put some fairy magic into the world: "Every time a child says, 'I don't believe in fairies,' there is a little fairy somewhere that falls down dead."

3. William Blake (1757–1827)

It's never too early for some good old-fashioned English mysticism. George Orwell mentions in his essay "Why I Write" that his
first poem, written at the age of five, was inspired by Blake's "The
Tyger." I now take much pleasure in reading that poem to the
children while they are eating their supper. Other poems in *Songs
of Innocence* and *Songs of Experience* are simple enough, too, for
children to get something out of, and all the while you feel that you
are educating yourself at the same time, allowing the "voice of the
bard" to knock around in your consciousness. And of course their
primary school teachers will be most impressed if your kids mention their knowledge of Blake at school. Blake was the great English defender of passion, then under attack from the new forces
of the Industrial Revolution and its "dark satanic mills."

4. Enid Blyton (1897–1968)

We can forget about Noddy, but the Famous Five books and *The
Faraway Tree* have stood the test of time. I think the appeal of
the Famous Five lies again in their independence. While Uncle
Quentin and Aunt Fanny hover in the background, the Five's
adventures are all unsupervised, unplanned and self-directed:
you do not get titles like *Five Get Driven to Chessington World
of Adventures in Their Parents' People Mover*. The Five even help
the adults in practical ways on occasion: for example, they foil a

plot by some criminals to rip off Uncle Quentin by buying his island because they know that there is a secret cache of gold ingots there. *The Faraway Tree* is like a computer game in its inventiveness and number of levels and lands, and its goblins and other strange creatures. Again, these books are available second-hand for virtually nothing. I love the old fifties red hardbacks of the Famous Five. They have the best drawings. Anne actually looks quite fanciable. The words simply poured out of Enid Blyton: she would supposedly write a 50,000-word Famous Five book in a week.

5. Raymond Briggs (b. 1934)

One of the few contemporary children's writers and artists of real genius. I could read *Jim and the Beanstalk*, *Fungus the Bogeyman*, *The Snowman* and, of course, the unbearably sad *When the Wind Blows* again and again, particularly *Fungus the Bogeyman* with its Beckettian nihilism. Every time you read it, you find something new. Briggs is a source of endless delight, and he has something to say too.

6. Lewis Carroll (1832–1898)

Lewis Carroll was the pen name of Charles Lutwidge Dodgson, who was also a mathematician. Inspired by the young Alice Liddell (a ukulele player) to write the Alice books, he filled them with crazy figments of his fertile imagination. Again there are no parents in Alice's world—only referred to as a hostile "they"—but the worlds Alice wanders through seem a satire on the messed-up logic of adults, with self-important clock-watching bureaucrats and absurd rules that defy reason. The Alice books tell us how ridiculous and confusing the adult world must appear to a bright child. All the adults are ridiculous, vain, cruel, conceited, sentimental, weak, bullying. Add to that some excellent poetry (it's worthwhile learning "Jabberwocky" by heart for use in power cuts) and John Tenniel's illustrations, and you have another work of genius that I could happily read and ponder from now to eternity. But even better to read them out aloud and practice your funny voices. I particularly like doing the hypocritical walrus in hammy Royal Shakespeare Company tones:

"I weep for you," the walrus said: "I deeply sympathize."

7. Roald Dahl (1916–1990)

My friend the writer and critic James Parker does not, in fact, recommend Roald Dahl to the idle parent for reading out loud: "Because there's so much damn SHOUTING in his books—it's exhausting!" But—with the exception of the lamentable *Charlie and the Great Glass Elevator*—I disagree. I've loved reading Roald Dahl to the kids, in particular *Danny, the Champion of the World*, although that book does have the downside of making one feel a bit inferior when it comes to being a Good Dad.

8. Daniel Defoe (1660–1731)

Rousseau, the anti-book man, makes an exception for *Robinson Crusoe*, written in 1719. He hates *Aesop's Fables* and any tales that attempt moral instruction. But Crusoe, he thinks, sets a good example to Émile: "It will serve to test our progress toward a right judgment, and it will always be read with delight, so long as our taste is unspoiled." Rousseau considers that *Robinson Crusoe* will stimulate a desire for practical knowledge: "The child who wants to build a storehouse on his desert island will be more eager to learn than the master to teach. He will want to know all sorts of useful things and nothing else." Rousseau, rather worryingly, does not praise the literary merit of the book; he is only really a fan of it as some sort of spur to useful activity, whereas the idle parent has a more "art for art's sake" attitude. It's also worth pointing out that *Robinson Crusoe* is very much the story of a loner: how does the isolated individual cope in a hostile world? Rousseau also, we remember, isolated Émile. But the idle parent, on the other hand, wishes to surround his offspring with people. We believe in community. The more, the merrier. Having said all that, this is a wonderful book and a pleasure for adults too.

9. Charles Dickens (1812–1870), *A Christmas Carol*

Kids can be introduced to Dickens at quite a young age, and *A Christmas Carol*, the classic attack on greed, is clearly the one to start with, read by the fire at Christmastime with all the kids arranged on the armchair of a kindly paterfamilias. Reading *A Christmas Carol* can also help the parents develop their own appreciation of Dickens (another example of a genius who didn't really go to school). What a fluid, sympathetic, imaginative and, of course, humane writer he was.

10. Arthur Conan Doyle (1859–1930), Sherlock Holmes mysteries

While Conan Doyle always felt that the huge success of his Holmes books rather deflected attention from what he considered to be his more important work on theosophy and spiritualism, we thank him heartily for providing us with so many good reads. Children's writer Michael Morpurgo reckons that *The Hound of the Baskervilles* makes the best introduction to Holmes. But all are great fun to read aloud, largely because the language is so clean and precise and there is a lovely vein of humor running through the tales. Again there is fun to be had with the voices: can you get Holmes' thin reedy voice? And shouldn't Watson be portrayed as less bluff and daft than the Watson of popular imagination?

11. Kenneth Grahame (1859–1932)

The Wind in the Willows combines magic with a superb satirical denunciation of the capitalist-futurist-neophyte figure in the shape of Mr. Toad. Toad today would be a computer addict, constantly up-grading and telling his friends about the latest social-networking site. Rat and Mole and Badger represent a more old-fashioned, providential approach to life, where ease and pleasure and plenty come to those who wait for it. Toad's addiction to motoring can also be seen as a metaphor for alcoholism. The attempts Badger and the authorities make to wean him off it and his wily escapes have all the hallmarks of the addiction process: Toad is a kind of Doherty or Winehouse.

12. The Brothers Grimm
(Jacob, 1785–1863; Wilhelm, 1786–1859)

Although *Grimm's Fairy Tales* are occasionally a shade too moral-istic ("And that's what happens to naughty boys"), I still enjoy reading them a great deal. I splashed out on a giant hardback with color plates by the ghoulish Arthur Rackham. There are plenty of bloodthirsty scenes: "Hansel and Gretel" still shocks, and "Little Red Riding Hood" is fantastically gruesome. (Avoid at all costs the sanitized modern Ladybird versions of these tales.) Again, fairy tales were a nineteenth-century phenomenon. Maybe their appearance at that time was all part of a Victorian plot to com-municate pious morality to children, and as such we "art for art's sake" readers should reject them. But I don't think actually that children learn moral ideas from such tales, however crudely the moral is shoved down their throats. I think they simply appreciate them on the level of a story. Therefore it does not really matter whether or not the story has some kind of moral purpose. Grimm's tales are clearly classics, and there is the sense that they have existed in one form or another for centuries.

13. Joel Chandler Harris (1845–1908), *Uncle Remus: His Songs and Sayings*

Harris, a journalist in the Deep South, developed a love of the tales told by slaves in the plantations and wrote them down. The stories are centered around the trickster character Brer (short for "brother") Rabbit. There is a nice retelling of the tales by the African-American social justice campaigner and storyteller Karima Amin, who seems untroubled by Harris's reported defense of slavery, preferring to focus on these lively stories rather than the political views of the man who wrote them down.

14. Charles Kingsley (1819–1875)

The Water Babies used to enchant me as a child, partly, I think, because the hero's name is Tom, a poor oppressed chimney sweep who turns into a little cherub with fins and joins a magical underwater world. Other worlds are clearly of great fascination to kids: think of Narnia, *His Dark Materials*, *Peter Pan*, *Mr. Benn* . . . I remember fancying, in a vague way, Mrs. Doasyouwouldbedoneby.

She was gorgeous. The gentle Kingsley, a radical Christian socialist, may be attempting to teach some ethics here. But I took not one whit of moral instruction from the book. I suppose it could be accused of sentimentality, like Dickens and many other Victorian works. But then Victorian literary sentimentality around childhood was no more than a horrified reaction to the Industrial system and what it did to kids. No previous age had had to cope with such suffering imposed on such a wide scale and with such methodical cruelty. This sort of radical proclamation of innocence starts with Blake, and I see Kingsley as following in his tradition.

15. Rudyard Kipling (1865–1936), *The Jungle Book*

Together with Oscar Wilde, we have decided that we are in favor of good writing rather than good morals. So we are free to love Kipling's *The Jungle Book*, written in 1894. As the abovementioned James Parker (page 229) writes: "The fight scenes are tremendous and readily apprehensible in their vigor even by the kid who is somewhat bamboozled by the lingo."

Choosing books of quality has the happy result of making you more well read. Through story time, you will become a fount of knowledge: your friends will ask advice on kids' stories, and you will begin to develop views and theories. To make kids' books interesting, you simply need to take an interest in kids' books. So you can no longer complain that as a result of having kids you have no time to read. Twenty minutes a night with the children will get you through a huge amount of literature.

16. Edward Lear (1812–1888)

What fun we've had with "The Jumblies," "The Pobble Who Had No Toes," "The Dong with a Luminous Nose" and "The Owl and the Pussycat." Children are fascinated by the fact that Lear was one of twenty-one children (his father was a bankrupt banker). I read these poems out to the kids while we are eating supper, and through repetition they start to recite bits by heart, a good skill to encourage as it both trains the memory and teaches rhythm and rhyme. Even little Henry can join in at points:

> Far and few, far and few,
> Are the lands where the Jumblies live;
> Their heads are green, and their hands are blue,
> And they went to sea in a sieve.

Lear's poems appeal greatly to adults as well, because really they deal with adult themes: love, loss, yearning and the desire to run away to a distant land. Think, too, about "The Jumblies": it's a celebration of single-minded eccentricity. When the Jumblies sail away all the people at home predict disaster: "And every one cried, 'You'll all be drowned!'"

But when the Jumblies return home and the landlocked

Victorian doubters see how tall they've grown, they change
their minds:

> And every one said, "If we only live,
> We too will go to sea in a sieve,—
> To the hills of the Chankly Bore!"

Lear is unsurpassed in rhythm and rhyme. He is the best,
and, again, you can pick up a paperback of *A Book of Bosh* for practically nothing.

17. C. S. Lewis (1893–1963)

The great charm of the Narnia stories, apart from the obvious
attraction of Narnia being a hundred percent parent-free, is that
C. S. Lewis essentially re-creates a medieval landscape, where
virtues such as honor, virtue, chivalry and courtesy are paramount, and where dignity and beauty are central values. (Lewis
was professor of medieval and Renaissance English at Cambridge
University from 1954 until his death.) The Middle Ages are tre-
mendously appealing to children, quite instinctively so, perhaps
because of the drama, passion and splendor of the age: they are all
over Disney films, and films like *Shrek*, for example. And there is
plenty in Lewis's books to amuse and delight parents. We've now
read the whole lot. What I particularly love about C. S. Lewis is
that, like Roald Dahl, he is completely unashamed about using his
books to express his own prejudices. He is particularly opposed

to progressive, non-religious schooling, which he sees as taking the magic out of life. Remember that one pair of children go to school at a bully-ridden establishment called Experiment House, where books about dragons are banned and the parents are vegetarian.

18. A. A. Milne (1882–1956)

The Pooh stories and *Now We Are Six* both offer endless fuel for speculation: are all the animals Jungian archetypes? Is Christopher Robin a sort of Christian God figure to the animals? Has Pooh got the right approach to life, just floating through like a Taoist monk? Should we feel sorry for Piglet or is his pathetic nature merely irritating? And why hasn't Christopher Robin got any friends? Is he in fact a sad and isolated character, seeking solace in his collection of furry toys?

19. Beatrix Potter (1866–1943)

Her illustrations are simply superb. Again, there is plenty of room for imaginative interpretation of these tales, which are sparse and never sentimental. Some, like *The Tale of Mr. Tod*, are really quite dark. It was Graham Greene's contention that Beatrix Potter, whose style he praised for its "gentle detachment," must have suffered some kind of crisis between the earlier, simpler tales— for example, *Peter Rabbit* (published in 1902, with 50,000 sales in its first year) and *Tom Kitten*—and the more complex and disturbing later ones, like *Pigling Bland* and *Mr. Tod*. "Miss Potter must have passed through an emotional ordeal which changed the character of her genius," Greene wrote in a 1933 essay. Potter refuted this suggestion, writing to Greene to say that she was not a fan of Mr. Freud's theories and the only ordeal she had been through at the time was an attack of the flu. However, a recent biography has suggested that she had been traumatized by the death in 1905 of her beloved publisher, Frederick Warne.

20. Tales from *The Thousand and One Nights*

Recently I was reading *Watership Down* to my children. Each evening I struggled through a few pages, regularly losing my temper because of the kids' inability to sit still and listen. One evening I allowed myself to be provoked to the point of throwing the book across the room. The following night I happened to see an old paperback Penguin copy of *The Thousand and One Nights* lying around, and we started to read "Ali Baba and the Forty Thieves." Two pages in I looked up to see three enormous pairs of eyes staring back at me in rapt wonder. This is the stuff! Precious jewels, caves, genies, bodies being cut into four pieces and hung on the cave walls, thieves being killed in boiling oil. There's a lot of sex in the tales, too, and wine drinking, feasts and dancing girls, and couples who "enjoy each other till morning." In fact, the tales give a good idea of everyday life in medieval Islam. The N. J. Dawood translation (Penguin) is probably the best, although the

Richard Burton one, while peppered with archaisms, is perfectly readable. Sensual, fantastical and thrilling, the tales also offer a satire on religion: every rogue claims that "it is Allah's will" when he is simply following his own self-interest. The final great thing about the tales is that there is not the faintest hint of Puritan morality: both Aladdin and Ali Baba are hopelessly lazy and shiftless. They become rich by pure good fortune. Things just happen: hard work is not necessarily rewarded. Fate can work in mysterious ways.

A word on the art of storytelling: reading from books or putting on a DVD has taken over from the old custom of telling stories from memory. The important thing is perhaps not so much the books themselves but the stories, and stories really are best told without reference to a book. The book introduces a barrier between the teller and the told. Sometimes, perhaps on a camping trip when I have lost the flashlight, the children have demanded a story, and I've had to fall back on my own resources and make one up on the spot. After the initial fear, you let go, and the story comes into your mind with surprising fluidity. The children remember such stories more intensely than the book-read ones. The other easy thing is simply to tell a story from memory, something like "Little Red Riding Hood," for example. It's actually more fun to do this than to read it from the text, because you start to add your own embellishments.

Philip Pullman puts it well:

I believe we should begin young with storytelling. We should encourage teachers to tell stories—I don't mean read from a book, I mean tell from memory, and I don't mean reciting parrot-fashion either, I mean having the story securely in your head till you know it as well as your own address or phone number. Every young student I have taught, I have encouraged to do this.... If you put the book away and it's just you in front of a class of children, in front of those thirty pairs of eyes, then you do feel very naked, very vulnerable at first. And all of them who did it said, "Well, it really worked, I was amazed...." Every teacher should have room in their heads to carry one story for each week of the school year.

We might read something like "Hansel and Gretel" and then memorize the component parts. We can also get the children to join in at certain points. What is interesting is that the kids seem to find it easier to concentrate when there is *no* book. The satisfying thing for the adult is the sense of fun and creativity. It's fun to perform your own bespoke version of the fairy tales, and it's creative to make up your own. The other night, I made one up for Henry about a big tractor and a little tractor. The little tractor never gets used to feed the cattle and sits sadly in the barn until one day the cows flee to a small field in the corner of the farm. The big tractor is too big to get through the gate, so at last the little tractor is called to help. They seemed to enjoy that, and the next day Arthur said to me:

"Daddy, you should write down the story of the tractors."
"Really, Arthur, do you think so?"
"Yes, and then we can sell them."

So now I have.

Finally, I would like to offer a tip for the parents: Always carry a good book around with you. This means that wherever you go, you will never be bored. I recently had a very successful idle parenting moment, and I thank the fact that I had a book with me. I arrived at Castle Cary train station with three children, but we missed the train to London. There was an hour's gap till the following train. I was filled with dread: how was I going to entertain them for an hour? Then I remembered my own philosophy. We walked into the waiting room. I sat down and got out my book. It was *The Doors of Perception* by Aldous Huxley. I started to read: "One bright May morning, I swallowed four-tenths of a gram of mescalin dissolved in half a glass of water and sat down to wait for the results." The children played quietly at my feet. After half an hour or so a lady sitting next to me leaned over and whispered: "I just want to say that I think it's wonderful that you are managing to read a book while looking after three children!"

So you see: Idle parenting works.

19.

Don't Fret
About Computers, or
Toward a Tao of Parenting

Perhaps, in the future, when machines have attained to a state
of perfection—for I confess that I am, like Godwin and Shelley,
a believer in perfectibility, the perfectibility of machinery—then,
perhaps, it will be possible for those who, like myself, desire it,
to live in a dignified seclusion, surrounded by the delicate
attentions of silent and graceful machines, and entirely secure
from any human intrusion. It is a beautiful thought.

Mr. Wimbush, in ALDOUS HUXLEY's *Crome Yellow*, 1921

Children are forgetting how to play. Or they are never learning in the first place. This is the great concern of those of us who worry about our screen-dominated age. Overstimulated almost from birth via the telly and the computer, children become accustomed to an intense blast of color, sound, music and words—and to living life at one remove. Frightened by neurotic parents who believe what they read in the papers and consider the real world to be fraught with danger, kids retreat into "safe" virtual worlds where there is no knee-grazing, no frozen water, no trees, no wood, no nails. Just a screen and a mouse and splendid isolation. Is this our vision of the future?

Well, I hate computers. I would rather use a quill, a pot of ink and the postal service. The first draft of this book, for example, was written by hand with an ink pen. But I'm not fanatical about my neo-Luddism. I use a computer for e-mails and sometimes for buying books. I admit I check train times on it and watch YouTube clips occasionally. However, everything that a computer can do can be done with more pleasure by the old ways. It is simply more enjoyable and more satisfying to write and receive letters than e-mails, or to speak on the phone than to communicate via e-mail. It is more fun and more pleasurable to browse a second-hand bookshop than to buy books on Abe. That way you may chance upon hidden gems or chat to the owner of the bookshop, who may be full of sage advice and suggestions. It is a convivial experience and full of adventure. Buying online is lonely, predictable and frequently frustrating. It is more satisfying and much faster to plan your train journeys with the help of a real timetable, and easier still if you go into the station and consult with the clerk. My small selection of reference books is far superior in terms of quality of information, and often speed of access, than Google searches or unreliable Wikipedia entries. Books give a physical pleasure, too, and you may stumble across other fascinating entries as you look up your particular reference. Books don't need batteries and they don't crash or lose their broadband connection when there's a gust of wind.

It seems that the geeks have taken over the world: the anti-social loner used to be a type to be avoided, but now he is a type we are all encouraged to be. The medium is the message: Blogs tend to bring out pomposity. E-mail is rude. Computers are in-trinsically geeky—afraid of nature, awkward in company, anti-sensual, ill, pale and lacking in style—and therefore tend to bring out similar traits in their users.

My other objection to screen worlds is that they are almost all funded by corporate advertising. This helps the world's biggest companies to grow yet bigger, as they are the ones who have the funds to plaster their brand all over MySpace or YouTube or Face-book (notice the Orwellian "Newspeak" quality of these names). The potential for small businesses is further reduced, and instead of risking starting our own small enterprises we are driven to set-tle for jobs with the big corporations. Screen-based lives tend to hasten the growth of the mega-machine rather than increase in-dividual freedoms—which was always the great claim of the Inter-net. From an everyday point of view, screens are bad because they create an infinite variety of wants in the child: "Can I have, can I have?" The stream of advertisements also encourages in the child, from very early on, a vague belief that it is best to be rich in order to acquire all this stuff and be happy. We should all work to re-create an age when children could play, when they were pushed out of the house at nine a.m. with a hunk of bread and were not seen again till suppertime. Even in my urban 1970s childhood, we would go out on our bikes all day, with no adult supervision at all. This kind of childhood creates resourceful characters. TV programs can be good, but are they as much fun as a picnic lunch in the tree house? No. Are they as good as sitting around the fire in the evening, telling stories? No! There are finer pleasures, deeper pleasures, and cost-free pleasures, out there beyond the screen.

In her unsentimental and dryly comic *Lark Rise to Candleford*, Flora Thompson paints a vivid portrait of life for the rural poor in Victorian England. Living on just ten shillings a week, they managed to enjoy themselves, and certainly their childhoods were more free than today's. It was a world of outhouses, no running water and a pig in the garden, and although they suffered from a lack of festivals and dances, the people were strong and happy. They had not been softened and weakened by civilization and an excess of comfort. The same applied to their children:

> Around the hamlet cottages played many little children, too young to go to school. Every morning they were bundled into a piece of old shawl crossed on the chest and tied in a hard knot at the back, a slice of food was thrust into their hands and they were told to "go play" whilst their mothers got on with the housework. In winter, their little limbs mottled with cold, they would stamp around playing horses or engines. In summer, they would make mud pies in the dust, moistening them from their own most intimate water supply. If they fell down or hurt themselves in any way, they did not run indoors for com-

fort, for they knew all they would get would be "sarves ye right. You should've looked where you wer' a-goin'!"

We may also take inspiration from the Yequana: "They do not make pitying sounds when a child hurts himself," writes Liedloff. "They wait for him to pick himself up and catch up . . ."

This attitude makes children strong, as was the case in Lark Rise:

> They were like little foals turned out to grass and received about as much attention. They might, and often did, have running noses and chilblains on hands, feet and ear-tips; but they hardly ever were ill enough to have to stay indoors, and grew sturdy and strong, so the system must have suited them. "Makes 'em hardy," their mothers said, and hardy indeed they became, just as the men and women and older boys and girls of the hamlet were hardy, in body and spirit.

These children would think nothing of walking three miles to school, or five miles to the nearest market town. Despite—or perhaps because of—their poverty, they grew up courteous and strong and self-reliant, a contrast to the pampered and spoiled children and adults of today, so often whining, self-pitying and rude. In those old days amusements were self-created. The children made up their own fantasy worlds in the woods and fields by day, and at night they were entertained by the storytelling of their grandparents.

Another problem with the digital world is that it yet further atomizes us and splits families into a seething group of individuals all silently pursuing their own interests through the medium of the computer. As Philip Pullman has said:

> Something else which is very salient is the fragmentation of family life, especially when every member of the family has their own iPod, their own computer, games console and television, and they don't exist as a unit at all, except by the virtue of living in one house. They all go off and do their own things, they don't talk. Most of their attention is not devoted to the unit, to the maintenance of the unit, the group, it's devoted to the gratification of themselves alone. And I think that's awful.

This steady process of the isolation of the individual from the community has been going on at least since 1535, when, following Henry VIII's smashing up of the old ways, we began the shift from being a community-minded people to being a set of brittle individuals each "secure from human intrusion," as Mr. Wimbush predicts in this chapter's epigraph. And our creativity and identity are expressed through our choice of purchases; as Penny Rimbaud writes: "I think therefore I buy."

We should be alert, too, to the language of computer software. Have you noticed how often computers "allow" you to do things? "This new Facebook application *allows* you to send a birthday card to everyone in your group." This makes the computer into a sort of authority, which gradually allows us to do more and more things—and we are expected to be grateful. The language of these programs, tellingly, lacks any subtlety and relies heavily on the use of the punctuation mark: "Invite Your Friends!" "Browse Through Pro-files!" "Get Started on MySpace!" Anyone who respects the written word, and indeed beauty, should be deeply saddened to witness the abuses that these computer geeks are inflicting on the language and should reject the Hobbesian worldview from which computer technology clearly springs.

But it's hard. Only yesterday Delilah said: "I want a laptop for my birthday." But she is six! What does she want with a laptop? No, no, no! I am not going to spend $800 so she can carry round a device that will separate her from the people around her and double as a shop that never closes.

The computer is an authority figure crossed with a device for securing new markets for global brands. Coca-Cola is more recognizable than a leek to small children. That's because Coca-Cola spends $2 billion a year on marketing. Coca-Cola is the world's number-one brand and it never, ever stops advertising. I'm always amazed when people say, "Oh, I'm not affected by advertising." If we really did ignore ads, then companies wouldn't bother to spend these vast sums on brand promotion. Imagine what good all that money could do; imagine the beautiful buildings it could build, and the gardens and parks that could be created, the seeds that could be sown, the bread that could be baked, the hungry people who could be fed. Imagine the works of art that could be commissioned if all that money that has been spent on advertising was spent in another way.

What practical steps, then, can we parents take to resist the tyranny of the computer? My pragmatic approach could be described as: "Don't ban. Minimize." The problem with banning is that of course it instantly makes the thing banned even more attractive than it was before.

Recently we have opted to limit screen time for our children to an hour a day. My original idea was half an hour. I told a friend with computer-loving kids our plan. Now this friend's son carries his laptop wherever he goes. "Half an hour a day? We're trying to get it down to half an hour an hour!" Once these boys played for so long on their computers they got laptop burns on their thighs.

In order to minimize, you need, as a parent, also to lead them into other activities—in a sense, to teach them how to play. Here is the great advantage, for example, of Wrestling Time. If I teach them wrestling, they will be able to wrestle each other when I am not there. Lately, after supper we have been going into the garden and playing French cricket for an hour, which is enormously enjoyable. What struck me was the huge amount of laughing that went on: I realized that people very rarely laugh in front of the telly or the computer. I find also that once I have set the children off on a game I can quietly sneak off and get back to my own self-ish pleasures. In a more natural society where the kids would have played in large groups, the older kids would have taught the younger ones how to play (as they still do at school, passing down hundreds of years of playground rhymes and games). Now parents might have to put a little more effort into teaching, if they do not want their children to be easy victims of the consumer world.

Computer games also cause arguments. "I regret the day that plaything of Satan came into my house," says my Belgian friend

Julie of her Nintendo Wii. Her two boys, she says, argue incessantly over whose turn it is and so forth. Computers divide; it is in their nature. Whereas something as simple as a ball brings people together.

I sometimes wonder how the consumer world can be so immensely attractive to children. Why, given the choice, would they rather shop online than go and play in the fields? Perhaps it is the endless novelty. Is it because shopping and online worlds give them a sense of control over their own lives, a sense that is denied them by their parents? Perhaps the computer offers children a vision of freedom that can be glimpsed from within their contained lives, rather as it does for an adult stuck in a boring job. Certainly there is undeniably something comforting about the screen: if Arthur is angry or sad, he will often be found on Rune-Scape. If that is the case, then we need to enlarge kids' freedoms continually. I feel sad when I reflect on the happy lives of the poverty-stricken inhabitants of *Lark Rise* and compare them to our cash-rich but conflict-filled modern family lives. What has gone wrong? Why have we become so pathetic, so reliant, so full of complaint, so anxious, so nervous, so fearful? My idle parent idea really is to bring back strength, well-being, fulfillment, satisfaction and happiness not just to children but to parents as well. Disappointed parents are the worst, because they get pushy, hoping that their kids will succeed where they themselves failed.

Above all, I think, we need to teach by example, not with authority. If we are happy, or at least cheerful and satisfied with life, then the child will naturally assume happiness to be the normal state. A manifestly unhappy parent telling her child what to do is not a very good advertisement for her own system. "If that's what you think, then I'm going to do the opposite so I don't turn out like you." Don't lay down rules. Then your children cannot be rebellious.

I am now in the golden age of family life. The baby years are over. No more diapers. Much more sleep. The children are now three, six and eight. We have a few more years to go before the trials of teenagers. I have reflected deeply on family life, made many mistakes, and while I am still confused, I am at least certain that I want to enjoy it, and that means first and foremost creating an enjoyable life for myself. The other things will follow from that. I am not waiting for a wife or a boss or a government or a child to make me happy. I am mindful of the importance of the present moment, because, in actual fact, that's all we have. All else is illusion. I have also realized that, particularly while the children are small, it is far better to be poor in money (or credit) and rich in time than vice versa. We will always be able to eat and to sleep in a bed at night. So I would rather be at home and go without a holiday and drive an old banger or have no car at all than work too hard and spend the cash. And there's no need to suffer: I am going to keep drinking beer, reading books and playing the uke. A life free from pleasure is no life at all.

ACKNOWLEDGMENTS

Many thanks to Victoria and the children; also to publisher Simon Prosser and agent Cat Ledger; copy editor Emma Horton; and all my friends for the inspiring conversations I had with them on these topics, in particular Heather Hodson, Dan Kieran, James Parker, Murphy Williams, John Nicholson and John Lloyd, plus Eefke and Julie, the idle mums of Antwerp, and Penny Rimbaud and Bronwen Jones.

Index